How to simplify your life

How to simplify your life

Seven Practical Steps to Letting Go of Your Burdens and Living a Happier Life

Tiki Kustenmacher
with Lothar J. Seiwert

and cartoons by
Tiki Kustenmacher

McGraw-Hill
New York Chicago San Francisco Lisbon
London Madrid Mexico City Milan New Delhi
San Juan Seoul Singapore Sydney Toronto

Editorial and production services provided by CWL Publishing Enterprises, Inc., Madison, WI, www.cwlpub.com.

McGraw-Hill books are available at special quantity discounts to use as premiums and sales promotions, or for use in corporate training programs. For more information, please write to the Director of Special Sales, McGraw-Hill, 2 Penn Plaza, New York, NY 10121-2298. Or contact your local bookstore.

 This book is printed on recycled, acid-free paper containing a minimum of 50% recycled de-inked fiber.

Easy is right.
Begin right and it will be easy.
Continue easy and it will be right.
The right way to go easy
Is to forget the right way
And forget that the going is easy.

—Chuang Tzu

Contents

Contents

Preface

Learning and Living a Meaningful Life

The book in front of you will become one of the most important books in your life. Of course, a lot of authors say that about their books. However, after many discussions, presentations, seminars, and intensive courses, we are convinced that this book will turn your life around fully in the best possible way.

This book is about the art of mastering life—unlocking the full potential of your life, leading to happiness and fulfillment. The traditional word for this is "meaning."

We are convinced that nobody can give you the meaning of life from outside; it is within you. You carry it within you like a bud. Living in a meaningful way involves developing your own potential in the best possible way and taking your place in society where you achieve the greatest development for yourself and society—the ideal balance between self-love and altruism.

If you follow the way of simplification explained in this book, you will find the meaning and destiny of your life. You will change inwardly and outwardly. Others will ask you why you look so happy. You will find new continents within yourself. You will develop strengths that you didn't even know you had. You will find a level of physical satisfaction that you didn't know before. Your position will improve on the material level. Having the amount of money you need is a natural by-product of the way of simplification. You will be valued and loved by other people and you will have an inner feeling of well-being.

The issue addressed in this book is a big subject, but that's why we feel able to make big promises.

The "way of simplification" is not just an expression—it means what it says. Many people don't find the meaning of their life because they ask questions that are too complicated. They don't see how simple it actually is.

If you have read this far, you have already begun the journey to simplification. We hope you find the experience very interesting and enjoyable as you take further steps.

Tiki Kustenmacher
Lothar J. Seiwert

The Way of Simplification

What Does Simplification Mean to You?

What runs through your head when you hear the word "simplification"? For many people, it is a positive term by its very nature. When they hear the word "simplify," they nod with a smile and a look of understanding. This is because they suffer from the complexity of life, from the dauntingly thick manual for their cell phone to the unfathomable mechanisms of the world economy that made them lose money on the stock exchange (although their friends told them it was easy to get rich with stocks). They suffer because of the unspoken demand for "more, more, more" in their environment. The excessive salaries offered in a big market do not mean liberation for a lot of people; on the contrary, it is a burden. They are weighed down by the steadily growing demands of their jobs, the expressed and unexpressed threat: join in or you're out!

When some people encounter the concept of simplification, they ask, "Why should I simplify my life?" They interpret the proposition of living a simpler and happier life as "something extra." Behind the concept, they sense a demand—"Now I've got to learn simplification as well!"

That reminds me of the old joke: "My wife cooks such good food; now I have to eat this diet food on top of it!"

Even though you'll find a lot of five-point programs and to-do lists in this book, simplification is essentially a non-doing. Simplification is the opposite of a demand. It is something positive, an ability you have had for a long time. Humans are essentially simple beings. Next time you're at the zoo or out in the wild, take a look at our closest relatives, the apes, and you'll see their magnificent capacity to spend hours on end hanging around, playing, and doing nothing. Simplicity in its basic form means just being.

Simplicity—A Basic Human Need

Strangely enough, practically all complex activities, inventions, and demands in our life come from the fundamental need for simplicity, i.e., this desire to hang around and do nothing. Everyone would like to earn a bit more money in order to have a safety net, assets that will allow them to live comfortably, with recreation and relaxation, in the future. People build a nice house with a garden so that, after the effort of building and furnishing and landscaping, they can sit around on the sofa or garden chair feeling content and doing nothing. The sophisticated dishwasher was invented so that we can spend time doing something more pleasant and relaxing than washing dishes. Building authorities came about because people wanted to resolve disputes (or even avoid them completely) so that we can spend time in a meaningful and relaxed way, instead of feuding with neighbors. Provisions for old age, household appliances, bureaucracy, and many other things in our complex world have been created because they make for a simpler and happier life.

However, in many cases we have lost sight of the good intention. The dream of a nice nest egg for old age has turned into an unpleasant battle over distribution among generations and income groups. Owning a home can become a full-time job. And we probably all have known about or even dealt with authorities who sometimes work against the people they're empowered to serve.

In a nutshell, the aspiration for simplicity often turns into a process of growing complexity.

The way of simplification endeavors to reverse this fatal dynamic and to return to the real purpose of our life. This purpose is the simplicity that reflects the fruits of a mature and fulfilled life. If you are in a confusing and complex phase of your life, this objective might appear paradoxical. But it's at the very pinnacle of complexity that the longing for simplicity reaches its peak.

The way of simplification involves opening up a new path in every area of your life and triggering a sort of "a-ha effect." It's as easy as that!

Reversing the dynamics does not mean going back; it's not a nostalgic trip back to the *good old times* or back to nature in the sense suggested by Jean-Jacques Rousseau. The way of simplification entails looking for the simplicity that lies before you and within you. This simplicity is conceivable only against the background of complexity. The way of simplification uses your life experience and the mistakes you have made. It's not something you can buy ready-made. It's the result of starting out on an exciting and distinctive path. It is the jewel at the end of a journey—although that doesn't mean that the journey is finished.

The journey goes from the outside to the inside. It begins on your desk, in your house, and with the organization of your time. It continues with your personal relationships, from your life partner to your parents, your children, your friends, and your colleagues. The way takes you to your body and your physical and mental fitness. And it ends in your thoughts and feelings, in the midst of your life and your personality.

Look forward to an exciting journey ... and begin your way of simplification with a dream.

Your Dream of Simplicity: First Night

You dream that an invisible person takes you by the hand and leads you out of the room you are in. A bluish-gray mist surrounds you and in the distance you see a glimpse of a new day.

It's difficult to say whether you are floating or walking or which direction you are going.

But then you see that you have arrived at place that is very familiar to you. An impressive edifice rises in front of you, like a pyramid, and you know that it's your own life pyramid. You can only guess at how high it rises, because the peak is still hidden in the cool morning mist.

The Step Pyramid Model

We can compare the way of simplification to a pyramid. The way to the clear, simple core, the essence of your life, takes us through seven steps that symbolize the various areas of life. The way upward represents the way inward. It works if you have at least one breakthrough on each step. The sequence is not the important thing. You can start at the bottom or in the middle or anywhere else.

Our experience shows that the desire for simplicity usually begins on the lowest level: the mess on your desk and in your home. That is why our overview of the seven stages of simplification starts with a very material subject, tidying up.

Step 1: Your Things

This means everything you own. Statisticians say that on average we each own over 10,000 things. However, the number fluctuates considerably. In your case it may be much more. You should make a start at your desk and experience the great feeling that you are coming to grips with your paperwork instead of letting it get the better of you. You then go on to your closets, the rest of your house, your garage, and your car, remembering to take the same approach with things at work as with things in your personal life.

Step 2: Your Finances

Finances are virtual things. It is frequently much more difficult to clear up money matters than to clear up the mess in our homes. After all, we are not just talking about cash and account balances, but also debts and loans and especially learned behavior patterns and mental blocks with money.

Step 3: Your Time

This possession is even more elusive. Every person has 24 hours each day. The real issue is just how much of that time is free, at his or her disposal. Wife or husband, boss, colleagues, customers, relatives— everyone stakes a claim to your time. On top of that, there are the everyday routines and duties, hobbies, and perhaps a secret passion. But where do you find the time just for yourself, to catch up with your-self, time to think and do nothing? Here again, you create some order and simplicity and, in doing so, take one more important step closer to your inner self.

Step 4: Your Health

Your body is your most personal possession. In many cases we pay attention to it only when it stops working properly. When people become ill, everything revolves around their body and they tend to tend to push aside all the other important concerns in life. The way of sim-plification shows how to prevent letting it get to that stage, with a long-term prevention of illness. It shows you how to achieve a healthy coex-istence of mind and body. This also involves a healthy relationship with your sexuality.

Step 5: Your Relationships

The social network in your environment can become the source of a terribly complicated life. Personal agendas, disputes, harassment, and envy are some of the harmful consequences. But even friendly relationships or social engagements can become complicated, especially if you let yourself be consumed by them, if you are only there for other people at the expense of your own needs. The process involved in the way of simplification clears up and simplifies your relationships. It frees you up for those human contacts that enrich you and help you to move forward. It helps to ease the relationship with your parents and other family members. In fact, it even helps you to see beyond your own life span.

Step 6: Your Life Partnership

The tremendous importance we attribute to love is based on the conviction that we come closest to ourselves in our relationships with significant others. The significant other does not necessarily have to be a marriage partner or a life companion. People with a religious orientation may find this relationship with God. For people who live alone, it may be relatives, friends, or other important relationships. The way of simplification puts an end to the nonsensical belief that career success must inevitably involve placing a great strain on your marriage or partnership.

Step 7: Yourself

The peak of the simplification pyramid is a room with a very individual character. Above the entrance is your life's goal, your personal idea of fulfillment and happiness, your life's purpose. At the end of your journey, you will find that the room is pervaded by absolute simplicity. And yet the room is not empty; it's filled with your own unmistakable personality. Here you will find much more than just yourself. And when you leave the room, you will experience a wonderful transformation.

The Simplifying Ideas

Every simplifying idea that we introduce to you is based on a simple principle: less is more. You achieve more when you reverse the spiral of complexity. This is why we say: reduce things by half instead of doubling them, get rid of junk instead of piling it up, relax instead of stressing, slow down instead of speeding up. Integrate these principles into your everyday life in a conscious way. You will then find yourself well along on your journey to simplification.

How to **simplify** *your life*

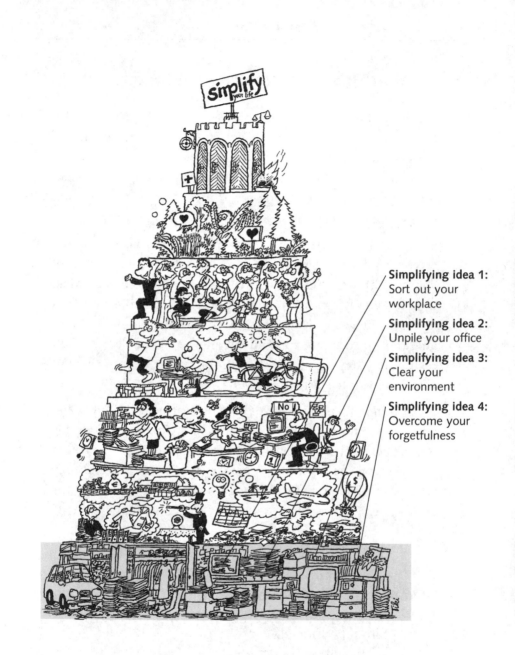

Simplifying idea 1: Sort out your workplace

Simplifying idea 2: Unpile your office

Simplifying idea 3: Clear your environment

Simplifying idea 4: Overcome your forgetfulness

Step 1 of Your Life Pyramid:
Simplify Your Things

Your Dream of Simplicity: Second Night

You are amazed at the size of your pyramid and you start walking around it slowly. In front of you, you see a huge quantity of objects, each one familiar. Furniture, boxes, gadgets, shelves with books, and closets full of clothes are piled up higher than the ceiling of the house. You see things from your home and your workplace as well as a car, a bicycle, and much more.

And when you see the large number of objects, you discover two conflicting feelings within yourself. You are proud of your wealth and the possibilities offered by each individual object—but at the same time the sheer quantity fills you with despair. You acknowledge that you don't use a lot of the things and a lot of them are superfluous and even troublesome. You realize that they are out of place in the edifice of your life. But where are you to start?

You find a place where you can breathe a sigh of relief and you notice a liberating sense as your chest expands. You decide to start here; this is the most worthwhile place. You now realize that you can move on to the next step of your pyramid only when you have put these objects into such good order that the achievement carries you upwards, feeling content and light.

Simplifying Objective for Step 1

Simplify yourself
with simpler things.

The lowest step on the pyramid is about "things." This means all the material around you: in your home, where you work, in your car. Most people sense intuitively that chronic untidiness in the home or stacks of paperwork on the desk is a symptom of a more deep-seated disorder. And they think, "If I manage my job better, then I'll come to grips with my desk." However, the way of simplification makes use of the astonishing discovery that it works much better the other way around: if you tidy up your workplace, in accordance with a few simple rules, you will feel much better. If you clear unnecessary stuff out of your wardrobe, your life takes on a new vitality.

For most people who lead a complicated life, the lack of simplicity is most apparent in the sphere of material objects. Most people who read our monthly newsletter *simplify your life*® have found that their most decisive step toward a simpler and happier life was to put a suspension file next to their desk or to make a consistent practice of keeping all floor areas clear. In your case it might be something quite different. We recommend that you use at least one of the methods introduced in this chapter so that you can get the first taste of simplicity and ease.

The way of simplification does not mean that every corner of your office and every room in your house have to be in perfect order. Far from it: start with one and savor the positive energy that this action generates.

Simplifying Idea 1: Sort Out Your Workplace

People can overcome immense difficulties, develop enormous strength, and devise technology to defeat great enemies. But they can accomplish these feats only one thing at a time. Anyone who doesn't know where to start will be helpless. The biggest stress factor for your mind is multiple tasks. This applies to everything we do. If you don't know where to start, you can't make progress. If you don't know where to find things in your workplace, you waste your time searching and you create chaos in your mind.

If you experience a crisis whenever you even look at your working area and if the chaos becomes an impenetrable jungle, you should initially use the first method we're introducing. It has proved its worth as an emergency measure thousands of times in particularly tough cases.

Incidentally, if you think you don't have time to tidy up your desk because you have too much to do, you should do it now! Even if it takes two to three hours (it rarely takes longer: people usually overestimate the time needed), the time invested will be worth it, because afterwards you will have a clear mind. You'll feel better and more motivated and you'll soon make up for the "lost" time.

The Four-Quadrant Method

This method has become known as the work secret of U.S. presidents and it was called the "Eisenhower rule." It has become popularly known as the time management matrix. This is the simplified version of the time management matrix for crisis situations:

Divide an empty table up into four areas. (Not your desk, but a table next to it or, if necessary, the floor will do.) Then work through the jungle of papers on your desk consistently in a clockwise direction and put each paper into one of the four areas, as described below, until not one single piece of paper remains on it. Make sure you stick to the task, don't allow yourself to be distracted, and trust that (after an initial phase when you may feel "I'll never manage this") the activity will give you enormous energy and enthusiasm.

4

The four areas are as follows:

1. **Throwing away.** The first area is for everything you can throw away. Ideally, you should put a large container there. Here is a list of unnecessary paper items, which should give you ideas for more things to throw away:

   - Old travel brochures
   - Newspapers over one week old
   - Catalogs over six months old
   - Magazines without any articles you need in the long term
   - Obsolete letterhead
   - Maps more than three years old or maps of countries you won't visit in the next two years
   - Papers from school or college
   - Old Christmas cards
   - About half of all the children's drawings you've become fond of (just keep the nicest ones—that increases their value!)
   - Wall calendars from previous years
   - Recipes that you're never going to use
   - Instructions for appliances you no longer have
   - Warranties that have expired

   You'll be amazed how much stuff is past its "expiration date"!

2. **Forwarding.** The second area is for everything that you can pass on to others to deal with. Here it would be great, of course, if you were the president and had the White House staff. It may be, however, that you have so much stuff on your desk because you don't like to bother other people and you like to deal with small things yourself. When you use the time management matrix for organizing, you have to get out of your habits and be quite rigorous in delegating work. Include everyone you can think of: colleagues, members of the family, someone from an agency that assigns students for temp work positions.

3. **Important.** The third area is for everything you have to do yourself soon. With each item of paperwork you put into this area, be clear about what the next step will be. Be really tough with this stack of things!

4. **Immediate action.** The fourth area is special: it is for papers that you can deal with right now while tidying up, by taking one of the following instant actions:

Telephone. You deal with the matter by phone, even if you had intended to do it by letter. If you cannot contact the person, put the document into area 3.

Fax. You fax the letter back to the sender with a handwritten comment (or mail it if the person doesn't have a fax machine).

Filing. You put it immediately into the appropriate box file or the relevant compartment in your suspension file. (More about suspension files in the next section.)

The Principles of the Time Management Matrix

The four-quadrant method works 100%, provided you adhere strictly to three simple rules:

- Don't make any intermediate heaps.
- Don't pick up any piece of paper more than once.
- Don't form any more areas beyond these four.

This initial process frees you up for further action. You have a free working area in front of you. You have tackled the heaps. Now you have the strength to deal with all the other places where the most serious form of material has accumulated: the pile.

Simplifying Idea 2: Unpile Your Office

The same principle applies to your filing system: your life will become easier as soon as you take to heart the basic principle "single instead of multiple." Avoid everything multiple.

The most familiar symbol for unhelpful multiple tasks is a heap of "to do" papers. Every piece of paper stands for a task that you have to attend to. But this pile of papers causes depression. It weighs you down because it's so dense. You no longer know exactly what it contains. Consequently, the heap becomes stronger than you. It silently defies you: "You won't get the better of me!" Furthermore, it's a mistake to believe that tasks are not forgotten as long as you have them lying on your desk. After all, once you've put enough other documents on top of them, they no longer remind you. It has been tried and tested many times: the combination of calendar (with a to-do list) and suspension files is the safest and most effective method.

A Horrible Stack

Stacks that have a depressing effect are not just stacks of things to do on your desk. They can consist of any of the following: unread magazines that you intend to go through later, interesting magazine articles that you're going to sort out sometime, vacation photos that you will organize into an album one day, even laundry in piles to be ironed. There are a great many possibilities for heaps in your environment.

The classical method of dealing with heaps  is to make sure they never form in the first place. "Pick up each piece of paper only once and deal with it immediately" is a clever principle that is possible with a one-time emergency action like the time management matrix. In real life, however, it is practicable only for the top people who have a team of motivated staff just waiting for something to be delegated. In everyday life, you will always have to store some things temporarily. So, heaps form inevitably.

The Suspension File:
Your Control Center for Simplification

The golden simplification principle for every pile of paper is simply "Rotate it!" Take stacks apart by turning each of the documents 90 degrees to separate them in the stack and then filing each of them in a suspension file, with folders open at the top. The dense stack breaks down into something much easier to deal with. It becomes "simple" in the truest sense of the term, because every task has a "compartment."

When you rearrange a stack using a suspension file, you're taking a decisive step. You're creating order, bringing things of similar types

together, and you can even create a hierarchy. For example, you can put the folders with the most important tasks right at the front.

What do you gain by this? Obviously you still have to work through your tasks, just as before. But you can file new papers in the right place, you get a proper overview, and after a while you'll find that the stifling feeling associated with stacks of paper is no longer weighing you down.

To ensure that you don't forget a task that has disappeared in a folder, you need to enter the relevant job in a to-do list, preferably one in your calendar or time planner.

Intermediate Station Instead of Final Destination

Your suspension file will soon become the central tool in your workplace, the control center where all the strands converge. But this is possible only if you treat it as an intermediate station. No papers should be there for more than about three months.

With discipline and a process of habituation, you can turn your control center into a faithful and motivating coworker.

Ten Tried and Tested Rules for Unpiling

1. Store in a box file. When something has been dealt with, it comes

out of the suspension file. The space there is too valuable. Papers that you need to keep for a long time must not remain in the suspension file; they belong in a box file. That is why there should be for each suspension file at least one box file that corresponds to it in terms of subject. Anything that does not need to be kept goes straight into the wastebasket. The "cylindrical filing cabinet" always has priority!

2. Create standing files. Things that do not belong in a suspension file should be stored elsewhere. Keep thick documents in a standing file. Put something like the cover letter for the document or a copy of the title page in the relevant suspension file.

3. **Log it on the calendar.** We've mentioned this already. To make sure you remember the task, make a note of it on the time planner at a realistic date.

4. **Invent clever names.** Label the suspension files with names that signify something (e.g., "trade fair stand," "research department," "business trips"). Avoid labels like "urgent" or "to do." Files with general, meaningless designations tend to become tombs in which important documents are lost. When you think about names for files, don't use unnecessary, stuffy official language; make use of the refreshing effect of humor. For example, instead of "To do" write "Answer me," instead of "Invoices" write "Pay me!," instead of "Appointments in other districts" write "Away from here," and so forth.

5. **Constant change.** Make sure that your suspension file is a living entity. Don't be afraid to keep changing the names of the files. For example, a TV journalist has a folder for every film report. When the report has been sent, the papers he needs to keep go into a box file and the old file gets the name of a new film project. Keep enough labels ready, preferably in the last compartment of your suspension file.

6. **React fast.** A method that has proved effective is to keep prepared letterhead and fax forms in one of the front files for quick replies. This procedure facilitates efficient responses.

7. **Consistent use.** Identify the type of papers that are always lying around on your desk because they don't fit any category. Create suitable files for them. For example, you might make a section for "children" (invitations for parents' meetings, class lists, forms for notifying of sickness) or "sports club" (if you are a member of one). Odd items that you've found (newspaper clippings, brochures) go into the relevant file. If none exists, create one (for example, "personal health tips").

Something that has proved useful is a "new travel" file containing all documents for business trips (travel tickets, itineraries, street plans, hotel addresses, letters of invitation, pages with important information torn from travel brochures). Information for each individual trip can be kept in a clear plastic folder. Before you leave, you take the relevant transparent folder and you can be sure that everything of importance is in it. During the trip, you can use the folder for all documents that you wish to keep, especially all documents required for travel expense claims. Since you have everything you need, you can even start the expense accounting on your way home. Then, when the trip and the accounting are finished, put a very clearly marked sheet at the top in the clear plastic envelope and put it in a standing file "Old trips." This is a simple and safe solution so nothing gets lost.

8. **Use the front side of the file.** On the front side of the suspension file, write telephone numbers, names, addresses, dates, membership numbers, and other facts that are relevant to the subject of the file. If you take the file out, you have all the important information at a glance.

9. **Be original.** Assume that your suspension file can organize everything if you manage it cleverly enough. Keep being creative in finding new applications. It's great if you don't just use your central interim filing system but develop a real love for it (and proudly demonstrate it for other people). Someone who loves writing with a fountain pen will have a suspension file with blotting paper, to avoid wasting time searching for it. A family man who works at home will have a file with surprises for his children (stickers, papers with puzzles from magazines, little plastic bags with jelly beans).

10. **Clear out material regularly.** Sift through your suspension file when it looks too full. It takes much less time than people think. Every file will include things you dealt with a long time ago. After 10 min-

utes of throwing things out, your files will usually be restored to full working order.

Don't imagine that you have to embark on some
gigantic clean-up operation when files are too full
and make your system perfect. You probably won't ever do it. It's better
to take a small step, but do it right now.

Alternative Filing Systems

Some companies provide filing systems that save you the laborious
work with classical box files. The process does not involve splitting up
and filing the contents of a file. Instead, the complete individual file is
kept in a special plastic container. You would, however, have to give up
your system of box files and completely reorganize your office.

The process you decide on is a matter of taste. This system requires
accurately labeling the file from the beginning, because the label will
stay with the content until the end of its life. The individual files are not
intended so much for temporary storage, but as an easily manageable
substitute for box files. On the other hand, in a suspension file with our
simplified system, over 80% of all accumulated documents are discard-
ed sooner or later. Only a fifth is filed in box files.

The thinner pockets have to be taken out in order to put documents
in them. The filing process is easier with the classical suspension file:
the file stays where it is; you just open it and slide the documents in.

Five Tips for Permanent Order

Whether you use a suspension file or box files, the contents will swell
inexorably. The time taken to find things will increase, information will
become obsolete, space will decrease, and your enthusiasm for work
will decline. But this is not inevitable. If you choose one or more of the
following methods of simplification, you will definitely be able to get
the flood of paperwork under control.

1. **The threefold rule.** Each time you look for something in a file that's
   constantly growing, take out three pieces of obsolete information.
   Remember that the principle of simplification involves small,

immediate steps. Have a sense of satisfaction every time a piece of paper lands in the wastebasket. It relieves the files, your mind, and your time management.

2. **Bartering.** For every new piece of information that comes into the filing system, throw out an older one immediately. Don't regard your papers as permanent property, but as guests that don't have to stay with you forever.

3. **Here-and-there strategy.** Each evening, put one or two suspension  files, box files, or filing trays on your desk. The next day look through them "in passing," while you're taking a coffee break, waiting for something, between appointments, or at your low point in the day.

4. **Expiration date.** Put a prominent "expiration date" on files or box  files that have no productive purpose after a specific date. For example, plans and calculations relating to specific periods can be labeled with "Trash on 12/31/04" or "File on 6/30/05." You can also put a throwaway reminder in your follow-up file or appointment book.

5. **The project celebration.** When you complete a task, go through all the relevant files and box files. Give back or throw away all papers and books you no longer need. Anything that might be needed later can go into a long-term box file. Then you can celebrate what you've done!

So Your Desk Stays Clear

We hereby declare the debate between the empty deskers and full deskers settled: the empty deskers have won! You won't manage to simplify your life with a full desk.

Here is the most important trick: keep everything that you've been piling up on your desk behind you. Set up a low cabinet, a shelf, or another desk.

The Desk Memory Book

Here's a good trick if you have a collection of scribbled telephone numbers and notes on your desk: gather it all up at regular intervals, cut out pieces of paper with notes, if necessary, and stick everything in a book with the title "Everything That Used to Be on My Desk." The advantage is that your desk is clear while all the information is still available if you need it.

Identify a Build-up Early On

If you don't keep up with the task of clearing things away, despite all the good intentions, it may well be caused by a small thing, i.e., a build-up that you don't notice at first because it's at the end of the line.

Here's an example. Bank statements are piling up on your desk, but the box file is full to bursting. You need to set up a new box file, but the shelf is full of box files, right down to the last inch. You need to completely reorganize the shelf and possibly clean up the whole office. However, you might not have time for that at the moment. The result: a lot of other papers start piling up. You know that the  important bank documents are somewhere, but you don't quite find the courage to confront the heap. It's a vicious circle.

Such vicious circles don't develop only on your desk. They can occur anywhere where things are kept, e.g., files and bookshelves, drawers, storage rooms, closets, and kitchen cupboards.

Deal with Current Problems Immediately

The key word for an organized environment is "flow." The problem is not that there's too much inflow of material; it's the stagnation caused by the slow rate of outflow. The difference between pushing pieces of paper around and real document management consists in making quick decisions. Most things in a to-do pile are not dealt with. They stop the flow, impair your motivation, and make you feel dissatisfied, rather like large items in the sink that block the drain. So get rid of them immediately!

Try to develop a sense for this type of build-up. Do a critical check. What is stopping you from organizing things at the moment? What is making you reluctant to do it? Is it an overflowing suspension file, a box file that's difficult to get to, or the fact that you don't yet have a file for new areas of work?

Remember that the principle of simplification involves small steps. You do not have to get rid of all blockages at once and you probably wouldn't be able to do so. But if you find one single thing that is causing trouble, then deal with it immediately. Don't spend time dreaming of the great solution; deal with the current problem as quickly as possible. In our example, this means setting up a new box file, even if it has to stay on the floor for the time being. That way you break the vicious circle and start a positive snowball effect.

Take Long-Term Action with the Three-Fourths Rule

Don't let chaos arise. Don't wait until there's a 120% overflow. Take action when your storage system is 75% full.

That means considering a box file to be full when about 75% of its capacity is taken up. A three-foot shelf should only contain 27 inches of books or box files. (To keep box files from falling over, you can

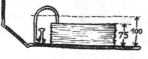

lay one of them on its side or use a bookend.) A hanging rod in a closet is easy to use only when it's no more than 75% full.

Obtain Successful Results with Step Files

We mentioned this earlier. The clever old rule that you should pick up any piece of paper only once is a great idea in theory, but in practice it's impossible. For example, if you want to fill in an application form that has just arrived, you may need to consult a colleague who's not there at the moment, you may need to look at old documents that are in the basement, or you may need information from the accounts department and it's not worth going to the department just to ask for that piece of information. In a nutshell, this means that one piece of paper turns into a complex process. These things usually land in a pile with an ominous heading like "Deal with later."

This is how the chaos begins. As American organization expert Barbara Hemphill puts it, "Clutter is postponed decisions."

The problem: There's a piece of paper in front of you. In order to deal with it, you need to address several matters at the same time. It's as though you see these tasks swarming around like individual beads that you need to string together. In the end, you put the whole matter aside.

The solution: Start threading the beads with the first one. Select one action from the many that are necessary and decide that this one is going to be the next step. In this way, each piece of paper that you pick up is taken one step further. Hemphill has developed a method for this that has proved very successful with her clients: step files.

Set up files in your suspension file with tabs in strong colors. Label these files with typical "next steps." These steps will vary from one job to another; in fact, they characterize your individual job. Nevertheless, some will be almost universal.

A few examples:

- Copy
- Present to the boss
- Phone
- Discuss with …
- Resolve with accounts department
- Awaiting reply

Here are the step files used by the artist, Tiki Küstenmacher:

- Create sketches
- Final drawings
- Waiting for the OK
- To be invoiced

Or a few step files for an insurance salesman:

- Fill in policies
- Send to head office
- Generate proposals

- Put in customer file
- Arrange appointment

The advantage is that processes of the same type are brought together. When you pick up the phone file, for example, you're automatically going to get a list of phone calls to be made in succession, a well-accepted organizational aid. Your desk remains clear.

Nothing is more detrimental to your enthusiasm for work than a cluttered working area that silently asks you, "Where are you going to begin?" As soon as you take out a step file, it's clear what is to be done.

Bring Happiness to Your Work Area

Keep your files in good condition, even externally. Keeping things in good order is more satisfying if you don't have annoying problems like file mechanisms that get stuck, labels that are difficult to read, or documents that are falling out. When you pick up a file or a box file, do

any necessary remedial work immediately (tears, broken tabs, faded writing). Don't leave it until the "next big clear-up action." (As a rule, that never happens.) Keep an adequate stock of separators, new files, spine labels, and folders.

Get quality box files with well-functioning mechanisms, attractive boxes, and pleasantly designed blocks of drawer files. It's worth paying for elegant containers for things that tend to lie around: a stylish diskette box, a fancy cup for pens and pencils. Take pleasure in keeping your possessions in good order and apply the golden principle of tidying up: everything has its place—one place.

If you can't fit any more into a suspension file because it's full to bursting but you can't get rid of anything, even with the best will in the world, switch over to a suspension file with a wide plastic or cardboard bottom with a greater capacity. Otherwise, you can create a box file.

Simplifying Idea 3: Clear Your Environment

Jettison ballast because you can only fly with light luggage. Useless things in the home and office are more detrimental to our states of mind than many people consciously realize. Your conscious mind has learned to ignore untidy shelves or rooms filled with old things. But your unconscious mind is overworked and weighed down by these things. It becomes free only when you get the stuff out of your house.

The Strange Effects of Clutter—and How You Avoid It

Chronic mess is not just impractical when someone wants to clean the room. An excess of things piled up at random amounts to an ongoing frontal attack on your body and mind. Over the course of time, your consciousness learns to cope with it—but not the unconscious. Numerous studies have substantiated the negative effects that clutter has on our lives. Let's take a look some of them.

Fear of the Future

If you are surrounded by more things than you can manage, you feel a weakness on a subliminal level. This feeling can transfer to other areas of life in which you would otherwise be fully effective. Clutter impairs your development, because things that are piled up are frequently associated with memories, so they bind you to the past.

Our advice for simplification: Think appreciatively of the people associated with the objects in your environment. Keep one very nice or valuable memento of each person and give the rest away. The memory of Aunt Doris will feel more special if you associate her with a beautiful pearl necklace rather than a whole cupboard bursting with impractical, old-fashioned china. If you have more room for new objects, this will make space for more future in your life.

Obesity

No joke: clutter can make you fat. This curious discovery was made by the British de-cluttering specialist Karen Kingston over a period of  many years: people with a lot of clutter in the house are often overweight. It may be that both body fat and material possessions can serve the purpose of self-protection. Obesity is often associated with "emotional constipation." In the same way that you can't let go of feelings and so you hoard old memorabilia, your body can hold back the metabolic processes and switch over to "store mode."

Our advice for simplification: Start with a diet for your constipated home. Kingston's clients have often found this easier than a diet for the body. That's the next step. One woman said that she couldn't keep stuffing herself in the empty home.

Procrastination

There's a similar connection between the chaos in your immediate environment and your motivation to work: disorder brings about procrastination. Clutter ties up energy and inhibits concentration.

Our advice for simplification: When you have a very large workload, the first thing to do is tidy up your desk and the space around it. The results will be more than worth the time you take, as you'll work more focused and faster and you will be happier with your work.

Regard your desk as a reflection of your mind. Whatever is lying on your desk you also carry in your head. A orderly desk is an orderly mind. Most people are amazed about their new energy after they've organized. Not only do they do their duties, but they also pursue their education, look for a new profession, come to grips with their relationships, or take a vacation to recuperate.

Financial Problems

Clutter costs money more than anything. Passionate "collectors of everything" say that they save money. However, it is a provable fact that a lot of their capital is tied up in things that they "might use one day." They are vulnerable to special offers and they buy things that they don't need at all. People who collect everything spend money on ways of keeping things— shelves, suitcases, closets, boxes, and even extensions to the house. Often they don't have time to use the things they collect because they spend the time on maintaining and storing all the things.  People who collect everything often live in homes that are too big. On average, 45% of the living space and usable floor space of a collector's house could be freed up by a consistent policy of getting rid of unnecessary things. However, the main way in which clutter costs money is that people with these collecting habits frequently stay in low-paying jobs.

Our advice for simplification: Tidy up! The best thing you can do is start today. We'll tell you just how to do it in the following section.

The Best Methods for Clearing Things Away

We are surrounded by chaos, ruled by the dragons of anarchy. That's how the ancient Babylonians saw the world. In this primordial mess, there is a tiny air bubble—the earth we live on. But if we're not careful, the chaos can invade everywhere again.

An idea that describes our everyday experience very well is that order is not a natural phenomenon. Chaos is the norm and we have to fight it every day. You could say that, according to Murphy's Law, any disorder that could possibly occur will occur.

A home where nothing is left lying around and where you could eat off the floor does not make for a simple life, because you spend so much time cleaning. It can even become a source of stress. ("Don't bring any more guests who don't want to take their shoes off!") Tidying up and cleaning can become an unhealthy obsession that can become the center of your life.

Simplicity means finding the golden mean between chaos and obsession: accepting a certain degree of disorder with an easygoing attitude but not giving in to the demons of chaos.

No One Is Born Messy

An excessive tendency to keep things is not a basic personal character-istic like being left-handed or having red hair. Many people describe themselves as messy and consider it to be a permanent trait. However, it is a proven fact that messiness is only a temporary condition, in some ways comparable to a slight obsession.

Every obsession is a search and every search has a healthy core: often people want to do something for others with their passion for collecting things or they have had a drastic experience of deficiency in their past. The only thing to do here is to be honest with ourselves about this tendency toward obsession and to work consistently to bring it down to a reasonable level, with help from some-one else if necessary.

A point of clarification: when we talk about messy people, we just mean people with a somewhat chaotic tendency. When collecting has become an obsession, it is detrimental to a person's life in a dangerous way. In fact, professional help is a matter of survival for these people as it is for any people suffering from an obsessive addiction.

Begin with Small Steps

It's better to deal with one drawer or one shelf section each day than to undertake some gigantic challenge ("totally clear out the cellar," "spring-cleaning of all wardrobes"). Divide the work up into easily digestible sections. Otherwise you will lose heart and the chaos will be bigger than you again.

Select *one* self-contained unit to begin with. A unit could be one drawer, one shelf, one filing tray, one box, or one pencil holder (you know, that thing where you put all kinds of odds and ends). What never works is "tidy up a shelf from left to right" or "keep on restoring a bit of order in a drawer."

Start with something that you can clear up completely in two to three hours: the herbs and spices shelf in the kitchen, a drawer in your desk, or the socks section of your wardrobe. The procedure then consists of five steps:

1. **All or nothing.** Clear everything out of the relevant unit (shelf, drawer, cupboard shelf).

2. **Make it shine.** Clean the empty unit till it sparkles and take pleasure in the fact that it's soon going to look really nice.

3. **The magic three.** Divide the contents (now lying on the ground) into three heaps:

   ■ *Wonderful.* Anything that is really useful and in good working order goes into the pile with this nice name. You put it where it belongs. But be critical: it must be really wonderful and have proved its worth. Ideally, it will be something that also has an emotional element—something that you like and use with pleasure. Here are a couple of proven ways of deciding what to keep and what to get rid of. Have I used it even once in the last two years? If it were stolen, would I replace it? If you find more than one of something (e.g., five pencils, two local telephone directories), select the best one and put the others into one of the next two categories.

   ■ *Real trash.* This heap is for everything that is broken or superfluous or that hasn't been used for at least one year. The things in this heap should be sorted into recyclable materials and residual waste and then disposed of properly. You could even make a box for a garage or yard sale if you have the time and inclination for this method of disposal or if you know someone to whom you can delegate this task. But do make a firm promise: anything that isn't sold the first time will be thrown away!

   ■ *Question mark.* If the decision about what is waste and what is wonderful is difficult, the thing lands in the "question mark" heap. These things are packed in a box (with a label indicating the contents!) and taken to the cellar, attic, or garage for stor-

age. Look through these boxes every six months. You'll be amazed what has been resolved in the meantime and how many things can be thrown out effortlessly. Things that have not been used for a whole year are automatically reclassified as waste.

Another method for moving toward throwing things away is the odds-and-ends drawer. Reserve at least one drawer in every other room for "junk." This is where you put everything that doesn't fit into any category. But don't pick a large drawer for it; use it sparingly and clear it out regularly. After three months, you will be able to throw away 80% of those odds and ends with a clean conscience because it turns out that nobody needs them anymore.

4. **Like with like.** Put small things together into boxes and other containers. In self-help groups for messy people, all conceivable types of containers are very popular, as well as partitions for drawers. Only with such sorting measures do you have a chance of lasting success with tidying up. Put the remaining things away again and mark new containers in large, clear writing.

5. **Hooray!** Take pleasure in the island of tidiness you have created—and don't grumble about how much is still to be done. Trust: in the same way that disorder has gradually spread in your home or on your desk, order can grow from the new beginning you've made.

Make Use of the Treasure Chest Effect

Buy professional storage systems. Don't economize here—go for quality. Especially for the desk, you should have a real suspension file with rolling carriages in a stand (not homemade solutions) and stable file cabinets (professional ones from an office equipment store, not wobbly ones from a furniture store). The reason for this is that you tend to accumulate more in cheap containers, because your subconscious knows that the storage space doesn't cost much. If you use systems that cost more, your subconscious does the sorting beforehand: only valuable things go into a valuable "treasure chest."

Look for Helpers

One of the most efficient means used in self-help groups for messy people is getting help from partners to tidy up. You will manage tasks that you keep putting off if you get help from someone else who's messy. He or she will have a realistic attitude toward the objects because, unlike you, he or she is not emotionally attached to those things. If someone has helped you, you help him or her. If you can't find someone who's messy, ask around in your circle of friends. Offer a supper in exchange or some other sort of gathering. The money it costs is a good investment because tidying up is three times faster with two people!

Renovate Your Home

Don't do this all at once, of course. Do it room by room. You will need to vacate the room—only temporarily, but completely. The method is time-consuming but very effective, because you are forced to pick up every object and make the decision described above—"wonderful" or "trash" or "question mark." One thing is certain: in a newly painted, tidy room, perhaps even with new flooring, you'll feel like a new person.

Become Aware of Surfaces

All types of tables, shelves, window ledges, and virtually all horizontal surfaces attract superfluous objects as if by magic. Even the floor, the greatest horizontal area, is an endangered area. Simplify your life by reducing horizontal areas and keeping the remaining areas clear.

The *coffee table* is a sensible place to put things during a coffee or tea break. That's why you should keep it clear for this purpose. It's a suitable place for flowers and candles (and sometimes your feet) but not TV magazines and the notorious coffee-table books left there to make an impression.

The *dining table*: nothing gets on people's nerves more than the laborious process of clearing the table before every meal. Teach your children (and yourself in the process) to regard that table as a "hot zone." It is reserved exclusively for eating (and possibly for evenings of card games and board games).

The *kitchen work surface* is, as the name suggests, reserved for work. It's much easier when you have enough space. Make a rule: only things that really are used on a daily basis (such as the coffee maker or dishwashing detergent) can be kept on the work surface. Everything else belongs somewhere in a cupboard; it can be set up quickly when it's needed.

The *top of the refrigerator* easily becomes a collecting point for anything imaginable. Put a nice foliage plant there or find some other way of staking it out as a forbidden zone so things don't get dumped there.

Enjoy being able to open windows wide. You have to keep your window ledges clear to do that. It's better to keep flowerpots together in stands than to just line them up on window ledges.

In bedrooms, chairs and stools used as "drop zones" attract dirty articles of clothing as if by magic. A better and more aesthetic option is the old-fashioned valet with a hanger, a hanging rod, and compartments for small things. People who are really serious about simplification store things they need the next day in a specific compartment of their closets.

The Simplified Room

You now know the secret of simplification: clear a path; you don't have to chop down the whole forest. Try out the principle of minimalism in at least one room in your home. Experiment in at least one room to see whether you can feel better without all those various "things." A very sparse but tastefully arranged room might have a very calming effect on you. For example, you can make the living room next to the very full, busy kitchen into a room with very few things but lots of room. Or you could arrange your bedroom so that it has a meditative, Spartan look.

Emptiness does not have to be cold. An inhospitable environment is created mainly by cold colors, materials that are too smooth, and lighting that is too bright and that covers a very wide area. It's rarely caused by the absence of objects. Ceiling lamps and floodlights pointing up at the ceiling usually give an unpleasant scattered light. It's better to have several standard lamps of medium height. Halogen lamps and spotlights should never point toward people's eyes; they should be adjusted as low as possible.

There's Collecting ... and Then There's Collecting

Everyone collects things: phone cards, books, matchboxes, small coffee cups, stuffed animals, elephants, stamps. It starts with a small display of a certain type of thing on a shelf and ends up spreading throughout the whole house: wallpaper, tablecloths, pictures, placemats, napkins, crockery, and even the collector's clothes are decorated with small frogs, bears, cows, or whatever. Behind this is an ancient human need to identify with something. It's often animals, as with the Native American totems. Collections bring a system into the unmanageable number of things that the world offers us.

Take a critical look at the type of things you collect. When did you start? What could be behind your collecting? Do you still have the need that you had when you started? Or does your collection bind you to the past? If it does, give it up. Normally, it's easier to give up a model railway or cup collections completely than to just reduce them. If there is anyone to whom you could give or sell your hobbies (and who would enjoy them), then do it! It will really simplify your life and free you up for new things.

Distinguish clearly between collecting and just keeping things. A real collection involves specialization and system, such as painted porcelain eggcups or calling cards from people who have the same first name or any type of teddy bears. Building up your own collection is a wonderful hobby that legitimately deserves time and space.

On the other hand, "just keeping" is an unsystematic hoarding of things that you could actually part with. You don't need them to live and it takes time and space to maintain them. These things can multiply until they control you. They consume time and energy, they take up room, and with time they become junk because there is so much and it's so unmanageable. There are a lot of motives for keeping things we

 don't need: respect (for those who have given presents or bequeathed things to us), provision for hard times, possible use in the future, the fact that something once cost a lot, or the idea that "this should belong to the next generation."

You should thoroughly sort through any things that you keep for any of these reasons. Instead of a random mixture of valuable and trivial souvenirs, you're then dealing just with a choice selection of things, a real collection that you can enjoy in a quite different way.

Give Things Away While You're Still Alive

The most popular method of getting rid of things is to leave it up to descendants. But the descendants find that nobody wants 95% of the treasured things even when they try to give them away. If you haven't yet gone through this experience yourself, let people who have tell you about it.

Go through your home and gather up all of the things that you're keeping for people. Then give or send these things to the people. (But first ask whether they want them!) Giving things away while you're still alive is one of the most worthwhile ways of getting rid of ballast.

Quality Simplified

Keep only the best. The poet Somerset Maugham once said: "It's a funny thing about life; if you refuse to accept anything but the best, you very often get it." Make quality a higher priority than quantity. Exercise a preference for the simple form that serves the purpose.

Get More Time for Living by Throwing Things Out

Above all, really go to town in throwing away old newspapers, magazines, and books. When you throw things out, do a little calcula-
 tion in your head; it takes about four hours to read a half-inch-thick magazine from cover to cover. Even if you read only selected articles, it still takes a good hour. A box with about 20 inches of printed paper takes between one week and one month—time that you can now save!

Even if this all sounds very theoretical, a shelf full of unread books or a pile of unread magazines has a negative effect on your subconscious. The thought is always there in the back of your mind—"I really ought to get down to that some day...."

A Decisive Factor: A Clear Floor

Things lying around on the floor are a sign of chaos. You'll be amazed how much more orderly your room will look just because the floor is completely clear. Full shelves, closets, cupboards, and walls don't look nearly as bad. The Shakers, a strict religious community in America in the 19th century, developed a culture out of this and they banished everything to the wall as a matter of principle. In all of their rooms they had pegboards where they hung brooms, clothes, and chairs (when they weren't being used). Items of Shaker furniture have become cult objects in the upperclass simple-chic culture in America.

Let that be an inspiration: use your walls to hang things like musical instruments, handbags, and other things that always tend to lie around. Pick an inconspicuous place if you don't like the sight of them, and don't develop an exaggerated sense of style—it usually looks more unpleasant to leave objects just lying around!

Your Home as the Mirror of Your Soul

Once you have begun the way of simplification in any room and hopefully been pleased with the result, you can go through your home systematically and optimize everything.

A basic idea associated with simplification is that your house is a three-dimensional representation of your life. There is a correspondence between your inner and outer worlds. People always leave invisible impressions in the homes where they live—even when they have moved out and all the furniture is gone. These impressions have effects on the next residents. Every religion has rituals for blessing and cleansing premises. For a positive living area, the most important requirement is to clear things out, to remove unnecessary things. Go through every room in your home and discover the connection between you and your living spaces.

The Cellar: Past and Unconscious

If you're keeping a lot of untidy things in the cellar, that's a sign of outstanding tasks that you're carrying around with you. You know it yourself: objects that you don't throw away because "they could come in useful one day" are fetters that bind you to the past. They may be an indication that there's something in your mind that you need to deal with: a burden from an ancestor, a dark secret in the family, or bad communication with a sibling.

Junk in the cellar can also have direct psychological effects: depression, listlessness, and melancholy.

The cellar is certainly a good storage place, but only for things that you use at least once a year. Arrange everything so that every object is directly accessible (not in such a way that the ping-pong table has to be taken out in order to get to the skiing equipment) and so that air and energy can circulate. A light, neat, well-ventilated cellar will make you more cheerful and confident and it will help you be in a positive mood. You will notice that you then have fresh energy to deal with the mental issues we've just mentioned.

The Attic: Ideas and Future

A crammed storage place blocks your personal and professional development. It acts like a lid that prevents your tree of life from growing. If you get rid of old souvenirs, keepsakes, worn-out clothes, and other things, you will discover new perspectives that you never dared to even dream of before.

A good converted attic is the best place for creative activities like writing or painting. If you plan to set up an office at home, the attic is the best place. The heads of big companies usually pick the top floor of the highest company building—rather like the way the top animal in the pecking order takes the highest place on a tree or rock.

Storerooms: Your Personal Freedom

If you have no cellar or attic available, one of your rooms may have become a storage place for all of the things that don't have a proper place. Such "dead" rooms in your immediate living environment are like a millstone round your neck. They impede your zest for life and creativity. Clear out those rooms completely or at least keep the storage areas clean and orderly. Ventilate the rooms regularly and don't keep the doors shut all the time.

The Entrance Area: Your Relationship with Other People

The impression that your home makes on visitors should be the one you make on other people. Use this trick: put on a jacket belonging to someone else, leave your home, and go back in again as though you were a stranger. Look through someone else's eyes: plants hanging down and blocking the way, an illegible name on the mailbox, a stack of wastepaper, an overfilled coat rack, and shoes, gloves, scarves, and hats lying around.

Keep the entrance area clear and make it inviting. You'll soon have new good friends and you'll feel better when you come in. This is very helpful if you want to become more open and hospitable.

Doors: Your Openness

Make sure that all doors (especially the front door) can open wide. Don't hang anything on doorknobs and use hooks on doors only if they don't keep the doors from moving freely. Never place closets, cupboards, or shelves in such a way that the door to a room can only be partially opened. Repair any broken doorknobs and oil any sticking or squeaky hinges and locks. Put a legible, stylish, and friendly nameplate by your entry. We've tried it: it's easier to work when the doors to the rooms are in good working order!

The Living Room: Your Heart

Like it or not, your self-image is influenced by the state of your main

 living room. A very sterile living room is no better than a chaotic or dirty one. Your living space should have a "center," perhaps a (coffee) table, where people like to gather around. Don't allow the television to become the central point in the room. Put it on one side or hide it behind a screen. You can use plants and decorative objects to keep people's attention in the room. Good light that isn't too bright and comfortable seats make everyone happy to be in the room.

Make a place for yourself there as well, where you can enjoy sitting alone—a place where you can feel happy being at home.

The Kitchen: Your Stomach

The place where you prepare your food has a special connection with your internal organs. There is no other room in a home in which the "turnover" in objects is as high as in the kitchen: plates, cups, glasses, and silverware are taken out, used, washed, and put away several times every day. Nevertheless, in the inaccessible areas of the shelves and cupboards, the turnover normally decreases rapidly. Unused dishes and food with expiration dates long past form a "clutter layer."

After completely clearing out the kitchen cupboards, people sometimes literally feel lighter, their digestion improves, and excess pounds disappear.

Dispose of everything in your kitchen that you have not used for a year, food past the expiration date, cups without saucers and containers without lids (and vice versa), china coffee- and teapots (outdated in the age of the thermos flask). Kitchen appliances that are used only once every two months such as the waffle iron or a slow cooker go to the cellar or a storeroom. The same for your fancy dishes or the odd assortment of glasses that you use only on special occasions. Baking utensils are used less often than normal cooking utensils. Make sure that the rolling pin, baking spices, and cake pans don't block the best places in the cupboards.

Freezer boxes, Tupperware, and other plastic containers have a tendency to multiply over the years. Take out any that have turned yellow or are broken or unused. Rule of thumb: you need only half as much as you have been hoarding. Some of the things you take out can be used for other purposes.

Put things together in appropriate groups in containers: e.g., sausage, cheese, and pickles for supper in the refrigerator; baking powder, sugar, and pudding mixes on the food shelf; honey, jam, and Nutella for breakfast in a basket; another one for teabags and teas. Under the sink you want one open box with cleaning materials and one with plant fertilizer.

The cupboards directly above the dishwasher are the ideal place for the dishes you use most frequently. If you have glass-fronted cabinets and you want to display granny's best china, forget it! This is where you put cups, small and large plates, pitchers, cereal bowls, and other things that are used continually. Here's the rule for wall cupboards: things used often at the bottom, things used less frequently at the top. The lower cupboard next to the dishwasher is for detergent and rinsing agents.

Sink, refrigerator, and stove form the working triangle in a kitchen. There shouldn't be any obstacles among these three points.

The fact that a surface is called a "work surface" means that you can work there; it doesn't mean that you park things there permanently. Hang as many things as possible on the wall, using adhesive hooks or screw hooks: scrubber over the sink, pot holders and oven mitts next to the stove.

The Floor: Your Finances

We have already made reference to the significance of the clear floor area. When closets, cupboards, and shelves are full, the floor frequently has to serve as a storage area. Stacks of paper, boxes, clothes, shoes, and all manner of things deprive you of your freedom of movement.

An astonishing observation: people with such cluttered floor areas almost always have financial problems. People who no longer have all

 the options of movement within their own four walls are restricting themselves and also reducing materially. Your "prosperity" is evidently dependent on the floor space available to you. Large, open floor areas always were a symbol for wealth; that's still true in banks. The bosses' rooms and desks are nowadays deliberately kept clear.

Take a look at the floors in all the rooms and clear them as much as possible. Devise new ways of storing things. Get shelving, standing files, and boxes. If necessary, set up new furniture and use hooks to hang things up. Don't have cables lying around. Bind them together or tie them up. A good way of doing this is to use the twist ties that hold new cables together in the package.

Wardrobes: Your Body

Many people who intend to lose weight keep clothes that are too small for them to wear again, even if they succeed at dieting. Experience shows that it hardly ever works. Do it the other way around: give away all the things that are too small and buy comfortable clothing in which you feel right just as you are at the moment. The best way to be successful in slimming is to have a positive relationship with your body. If you hate your stomach, it will stay out of sheer defiance.

This is how you simplify your wardrobe. Use the following tips as a checklist and start sorting, preferably immediately, in front of your open closet.

The best quarter. Hang all the things that you have worn often in the last eight weeks at the far left on the hanging rod; pullovers, T-shirts, etc.

 that you wear frequently go into a special compartment. This includes items that are not suitable for the current season, provided that you could say, "I would wear that right now if it were warm (or cold) enough outside." The items of clothing that you select in this way are your favorite things. They seldom take up more than a quarter of your closet.

The waste of space. There is a 98% probability that you will never again wear anything that you haven't worn in over one year. You're giving up too much room for these undesirable items in your wardrobe. So, weed them out! Even if something was once expensive or if it was a gift from someone close, it has served its purpose and it can go (into a container for donation, to a second-hand shop, to be given away, or into a wastebasket).

The new beginning: Now the creative part begins. Examine each of your favorite things from the "best quarter" very carefully. What makes it so wearable for you? Is it the cut, the size, the color, the material? This gives you the criteria for a personal simplification program so you can build up your wardrobe systematically.

Don't go for extravagant items that people quickly get tired of. Get single-color combinations that you can wear on all sorts of occasions. Invest in your daily clothing instead of special clothes that you wear only occasionally. The simplified basic wardrobe is conventional and it's not geared to  one particular season. However, when it comes to accessories (ties, scarves, jewelry), you can go with the fashions and even set new trends.

The Bathroom: Your Inner Center

The space where you take care of your body should be an environment in which you can be centered and undisturbed. Keep the many bottles, tubes, and other typical bathroom things behind doors and arrange the free space with plants and other things that you like. New towels in a nice color are the most cost-effective bathroom decoration.

The Bedroom: Your Intimacy

Traditionally, the bedroom is the place in a house that is taboo for guests. That is why it is frequently misused as a storage room for everything that would be a nuisance anywhere else. And yet it's in that room where you spend the night that you need harmony and order. Get rid of the classic sources of negative emotion: dirty laundry, boxes with old things, and broken objects. Don't store anything under the bed except perhaps bed linens and blankets. Take a look through drawers as well. Nobody needs 40 pairs of socks or 15 old-fashioned pullovers. A neat bedroom will allow you deeper sleep and often a more intensive love life.

The Garage: Your Mobility

If your garage is so full that you have to park your expensive car out-side just to keep your skis, wheelbarrows, and surfboards warm and dry, this should set off an alarm for you. You're "stuck." A basic rule: the easier it is to put your car into the garage, the greater the mobility of your mind and body.

There's no better place than the garage to apply the Shaker principle in a really consistent way. Hang as much as possible on the walls. Tires, roof racks, tools, containers, cleaning materials, and many other things are best kept on shelves.

Portable Junk: Your Burden

Briefcases, handbags, pants pockets—the more fully you pack them, the more clearly they symbolize all of the burdens that weigh your life down. If you're embarking on a cleaning-up operation, go through your pockets. You should be traveling light in your everyday life.

Try something small to begin with—your *purse*. Take out old receipts, obsolete check cards, etc. Don't carry too many coins around with you. Arrange your dollar bills by denomination. This will help you to bring order into all your financial affairs. Always act in accordance with the principle that external things affect what goes on within you.

To bring about long-term order in handbags and briefcases, you need to divide the contents into sensible, individual modules. Here are the six most important ones.

Module 1: Purse. In addition to bills and coins, purses sometimes con-tain credit cards, check cards, a driving license, and (in some countries) an ID card.

Module 2: Emergency case. You can have a bag with a zip fastener with typical first aid items, e.g. headache tablets, lip balm, eye drops, bandages, pocket-knife, a sewing kit from a hotel, and a toothbrush.

Module 3: Special children's bag. Another bag with a pacifier, a small toy, little cookies, children's bandages, antiseptic cream, or other useful things for when you take the kids out.

Module 4: Mini office. Most simply in the form of a time planner or an electronic organizer in a case that has additional space. It should also include a pen, Post-it® notes, stamps, pocket calculator, cellophane tape (a very practical option is Scotch® Tape Strips™, which work without a dispenser).

Module 5: Key ring. The smaller, the better. If you want it to make it bigger to make it easier to find, don't use loads of fancy stuff. It's better to have a attractive leather key case that doesn't wear out your bag or pants pocket. However, once you've divided the contents of your bag into modules, the key ring no longer has to be particularly prominent for you to find it easily.

Module 6: Cell phone. This is a module in itself. Some modern handbags and briefcases have a special compartment for a cell phone. If you use it, you won't need an unwieldy protective cover for your cell.

With the help of these clearly separated units, you can quickly switch over from one bag to another. As the individual bags have a limited capacity, you notice immediately if too much unnecessary stuff has accumulated in any of them and you sort it out.

The biggest advantage of the module system is that you only have to take with you the modules that you actually need. Here are a few examples:

- Shopping: modules 1, 5, and possibly 6.
- Major shopping expeditions with children: 1, 3, and 5.
- A business appointment: 1, 2, 4, 5, and 6.

■ Going out in the evening: 1, 3, 5. (6 remains handy for emergency calls, preferably in the glove compartment of your car. Cell phones tend to be a nuisance for everyone in movie theaters, restaurants, and concert halls.)

The Staircase: Your Opportunities for Growth

If you live in a multi-story building, you'll know the little piles of things that accumulate on the landings. People leave things there that they intend to take up the next time they go. These heaps can become a source for more disorder to erupt. In chaotic buildings, the stairs can degenerate and become a big storage area. The secret message to your inner mind is that the "way up" is blocked. It's just like the cluttered floor: you unconsciously block off new opportunities.

Make an agreement with all the residents that objects may be placed on the stairs only if they're to be taken to the next floor as soon as possible. Anyone whose hands are free must take whatever is on the stairs.

In the kitchen, use the "cellar basket" trick. Place a large basket with a handle there and agree that everything that's to be taken to the cellar will be put into the basket (empty bottles, materials for recycling, laundry, food for the pantry, etc.). You also need to agree with everyone that whoever goes down to the cellar next takes the full basket and puts the contents where they belong. This system also has the advantage that the person can use the basket to carry up the things he or she has gone to the cellar to collect.

Important Tips for Tidying Up

Find a place for everything. *Operating instructions* that you'll probably keep using (e.g., for the fax or video recorder) are best kept under the device. This is a real time saver. Put instructions that you use only occasionally in the file for devices and appliances—just an ordinary file with compartments for manuals. In each compartment you put the receipt and warranty for the device or appliance you've just bought (camera, toaster, refrigerator, vacuum, telephone, etc). Cut up the instructions and keep just the section in English. This is a tip that really saves space.

If buttons or switches have unintelligible symbols, use labels with more detailed information. You can write with a soft pencil on most plastic casings. A longer-lasting solution is to use a permanent marker pen. (You can later remove the ink with petro-leum-based cleaning fluid.)

A proven method is to use large numbers that indicate the sequence of buttons to be used. On an espresso machine, this could be: 1. Switch on; 2. Put cup underneath; 3. Press coffee button; 4. Switch off.

The Six Golden Rules for Keeping Things in Good Order

Simplification and order are great as long as you maintain them. In the initial period, stick the following six rules for simplification and order in a prominent position on your bulletin board, if necessary in every space that you want to simplify:

1. If you take something out, put it back.

2. If you open something, close it afterwards.

3. If something falls down, pick it up.

4. If you take something down, hang it up again.

5. If you intend to buy something later, write it down at once.

6. If you need to repair something, do it within a week.

Get Rid of Your Expectations

Perfectionism remains one of the most serious blockages for a happy, relaxed, orderly life. You are a human being and you naturally have a lim-ited capacity. American expert Barbara Hemphill points out that the prob-lem with disorderly people is not so much the lack of organization but the lack of perspec-tive. These people have a sort of tunnel vision. They just see what they *ought* to do, and that obscures their view of what they *can* do. Consequently, they lack the energy to deal with tasks in the present. They lose the bigger picture of the future, the enthusiasm associated with possibilities and surprises, the wider horizon of people who are mentally awake and free. Every pile or other collection of things that *have* to be done obscures this horizon for you.

Simplifying Idea 4:
Overcome Your Forgetfulness

90% of all people regularly have to search for lost objects. This fact was revealed by a study conducted by the opinion research institute EMNID in Bielefeld, Germany, on behalf of *simplify your life®*. The item people search for most is keys: 42% of those questioned said they are irritated again and again by having to search for their keys. Ballpoint pens take second place on the list of missing things (almost 25%). Third come eyeglasses (19%), while purses take fourth place (16%). People under 30 look for keys much more frequently than older people. The object most commonly mislaid by people over 50 is glasses (over 40%). There are no great differences between men and women. Women have more trouble finding their purses, but they look after their keys a little better than the men.

In any case, it's a waste of time and it has negative effect on our moods if we create stress by unnecessary searching. Forgetfulness with small things is not some unalterable natural phenomenon. In this area, too, you can simplify your life significantly with a little effort.

A Mental System to Make Sure You Find Things

What can we do? The most promising thing is the principle of order according to which each thing has its specific place. Many people have resolved to put their keys in a particular place whenever they come into the house—but they don't stick with that resolution consistently. The problem is that the specific place has not become established deep enough in the brain. A combination of memory-friendly learning methods can help here.

Unique location. Find a definite place near the front door. It might be a drawer, a keyboard with hooks or pegs, a key box, a bowl on a table, or another easily accessible place. You can do the same thing in your office.

Unique color. Mark the location with a conspicuous new color. Put colored adhesive tape along the outside of the drawer handle, paint the keyboard in a different color, or replace the bowl with a different-colored one. This will anchor the location in the right side of the brain, which operates in images and is particularly receptive to colors.

Unique name. Give the place an unmistakable name: "the blue drawer" (provided it's the only blue drawer in your home), "the pink pig board" (a funny name sticks particularly well), "the star bowl" (because it's decorated with very prominent star patterns). The name anchors the location in the analytical left hemisphere of the brain, which is also good with letters. Excessively complex names are not favorable ("the top left drawer in the chest of drawers next to the front door").

Using a succinct name means you can give others instructions ("put the key in the star bowl!") and when you're under stress or pressed for time you'll manage ("key—blue drawer!").

Positive emotions. The success of this small action can become even greater if the organizing process itself is associated with a pleasant feeling. For example, put a bit of potpourri (leaves suffused with aromatic oil) in the key box that gives off a fragrance that you like. Or you can lay material that you like in your key drawer, perhaps red silk, so the key will land softly when you throw it into the drawer.

Everything Has Its Place

Develop unique storage principles for other articles that are often misplaced, such as purses, glasses, or ballpoint pens. A few options:

- Make it a principle that "the purse always stays with the keys." When you come home, it also lands in the key drawer.
- Keep your glasses on you at all times (in a shirt pocket, in your handbag, or on a chain around your neck).
- Keep pens handy in a cup next to the phone. Put a pen in each briefcase and handbag and keep it there. There should also be a pen or a pencil in the glove compartment of your car.

Trips

On vacation or business trips, it is even more important than at home that you keep purses, hotel keys, ID cards, etc. on you at all times and that you have a place for everything in the unfamiliar environment of the hotel room. Get into the habit of selecting a definite place for your important things when you first enter a hotel room and then putting things there immediately. Places that prove useful include the top of the bedside table, the bedside table drawer, the desk drawer, or (if you're worried that strangers will see your things and steal them) a compartment in your suitcase, which you then keep open. Valuables (large quantities of cash, real jewelry), of course, belong in the hotel safe.

To make sure that you have all of your important things when you leave the hotel room, you should work out a definite system for where you keep the things that you take with you. Here are a few options that have been found to work:

The heart method

The most important things can be "over your heart." In the inside left jacket pocket is the wallet (with cash, check card, credit cards, ID card, telephone card, and driving license).

On train trips you can also keep the tickets over your heart in your shirt pocket. The shirt pocket is also a good place for tickets for parking ramps or for public transportation for which people often can't quite find the "right" place.

In the inside right jacket pocket you keep your passport. This pocket is also a good place for airline tickets. In the outside right jacket pocket you can keep coins or small bills of the local currency, so they're convenient for tips.

Women can either keep all these things in their handbag or likewise wear a jacket with various pockets (like the American master of simplicity, Elaine St. James).

Travel light. All other travel documents that you don't need constantly during the trip (hotel coupons, vaccination certificates) can be kept in your travel bag. If it's a shoulder bag, you should protect your back by always wearing the strap diagonally (even if it doesn't look so nice). Or better still, use a backpack.

On long journeys you can keep your keys (which you need only when you return home from your trip) in a secure compartment in the travel bag from the very beginning. It would be ridiculous to walk around foreign cities with your own house keys in your pants pocket!

Finding the hotel key quickly. The left outside pocket is reserved for the hotel key. For reasons of security, it is advisable to always take the key with you instead of leaving that at the reception desk. If necessary, take off the gigantic tag and leave it in the room. If you get a card instead of a key, it's best to keep it in a purse with your credit cards. If the hotel gives you a security card, you should keep it separate from the key card.

A little extra tip: as a matter of principle, always take a business card from the reception desk when you check in and keep it carefully. That way you will always find your way back to the hotel. If you're in a country where they don't speak your language, you can show the address to the taxi driver (particularly important in areas that don't use the Roman alphabet, like Asia and the Middle East). If you realize after your departure that you've left something in the room, you'll have the hotel's phone number handy.

When it comes to mislaying things, the principle is "A danger foreseen is half avoided." As soon as you decide to do something to escape your daily search for your keys and purse, you have already managed the first important step. And you have made significant progress on the path of simplification. You are no longer a slave to your possessions—you do what *you* want with them.

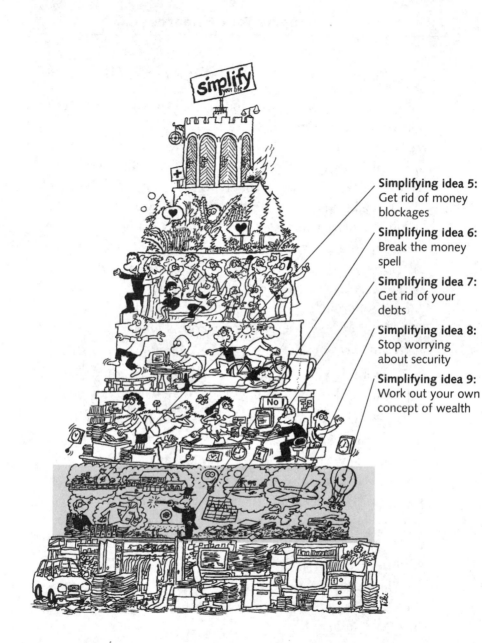

Simplifying idea 5:
Get rid of money blockages

Simplifying idea 6:
Break the money spell

Simplifying idea 7:
Get rid of your debts

Simplifying idea 8:
Stop worrying about security

Simplifying idea 9:
Work out your own concept of wealth

Step 2 of Your Life Pyramid:
Simplify Your Finances

Your Dream of Simplicity: Third Night

You've found a good place on the first step of your pyramid and opened up a path through the mess that had seemed impenetrable before. To your surprise, you discover a convenient staircase in the place that you've opened up and you climb with confident steps. You're curious about what the next step will look like. You had expected it not to look much more tidy here than below, but what you now see renders you speechless. It's like being on an emotional roller coaster as you walk around this second story. One moment you like it, you feel happy and euphoric, and then you're gripped with horror. You feel fear and horror, guilt and redemption, suspense, and then weary boredom. First you're daring and courageous; then you feel hesitant and cautious again.

Everything you see appears real and, at the same time, an ideal, rather like the changing images on a television screen.

It's as though you're coming very close to your dreams on this step of your life pyramid. Your longings and desires seem to reside here, and sometimes it seems as though they could be fulfilled quickly here—and then they seem indescribably far away again. What is this dream about? It's about happiness and comfort, hope and fear, miserliness and extravagance. You sense that money is the subject of this story, but you had imagined going around this territory very differentl—objectively and devoid of feeling.

The shelves are full of money and bank statements, stocks, and check cards. But you notice that this territory is only marginally about hard facts.

Simplifying Objective for Step 2

Learn how to achieve financial independence without complexes.

In the world of physical objects, junk is what lies around and hinders your development; when it comes to money, it's your thoughts and feelings about money that do the same thing.

Simplifying Idea 5:
Get Rid of Money Blockages

A public opinion research institute in Germany has been asking a representative cross-section of German society about their experiences since 1955. In response to the question "Are you happy?" 30% of the people questioned consistently replied, "Yes," despite the rising standard of living. In the list ranking answers to the question "What is important for my happiness?" money has occupied the top place for decades. 80% of Germans regard freedom from money concerns to be a requirement for a happy life.

"When I'm rich, then I'll be happy!" That's a statement that normally makes people unhappy. If you are unhappy now and hope to become happier in the future through more money, then you're hoping in vain. The simplification advice is to turn the old sequence of happiness and wealth around: "If I am happy, I have a chance of becoming rich." A Tibetan saying gives an indication of the proper measure of wealth: a person is rich when he knows that he has enough.

Buy things that really mean something to you—and wait until you have enough money. Most people waste too much time wishing that life were different from how it actually is. The key to happiness is in being able to enjoy what you've got, even if it doesn't look like much from the outside.

Develop Equanimity

When it comes to finance, the way of simplification contains an apparent paradox: you can earn more money only if you can let go of it. As soon as you cling to money, the way to wealth is blocked.

Letting go is, however, not the same thing as indifference. Many people say things like "I don't care about money." In this way, they set up a block in relation to wealth: "I don't really want money." A person with equanimity says, "I'm going to work hard and take every opportunity to use my abilities to become successful. But if it doesn't work, I can live with it."

Have Courage

Think courageous thoughts and write them in bold statements: "Yes, I have debts, but millions of people have managed to pay off their debts and I can do it as well. There are many people with capabilities similar to mine and they earn much more than I do. I shall soon join them."

Change your language when it comes to money and earning:

Do not say …	Instead say …
I can't …	*I can* …
I don't know how to …	*I'll learn how to* …
I wish I …	*I will have* …

Discover Your Mental Barriers

You have discovered the most important blockages in your heart and

got rid of them as far as possible. As a next step, you should now work out which blocks are lurking in the back of your mind in relation to money and wealth. Here are the four most common hurdles in our thoughts and judgments.

Things Our Parents Said

We carry around a whole range of wise old sayings on a subconscious level, because they have been instilled in us: "You can't become rich by honest means," "People who come into money lose their friends," "Money can't buy happiness," and many other sayings that have comforted badly paid workers for centuries. "Wealth" has thus become a negative concept for a lot of people, even though they may appreciate the advantages of prosperity.

Our advice for simplification: Don't talk about "wealth" or "a lot of money." Use the expression "financial independence" instead.

What-if Worries

"What happens if I become unemployed?" "What if the business we've set up fails?" People who spend time thinking about failure will indeed soon fail. Almost all successful business people have begun by giving something up and plunging into a daring exploit. But they weren't thinking about failure; they had a great vision.

Our advice for simplification: Have a clear, attractive image in your mind—a positively formulated life aim that you want to achieve.

The Lottery Dream

Careful! There are visions that create blockages. These include dreams of great fortune—the idea of being discovered as a star, winning the lottery, or inheriting an unknown uncle's estate. The problem with such fantasies is that they don't inspire you to take any action. On the contrary, they condemn you to passive waiting and hoping.

Our advice for simplification: Stop spending on lotteries and other forms of gambling. Instead, resolve to earn that $5,000 (or more) within one year as you might get if you were lucky enough to win a moderate lottery prize. Biographies of successful people are full of accounts of additional jobs: driving a taxi, delivering newspapers, writing books, conducting seminars, etc. Even if much of these accounts seem to have been glorified into legends, one thing is clear: successful people have always been doers and they have never been content with the role of victims.

Excuses

Excuses are sentences like "I would like to ..., but ...." Think about it:

both halves of the sentence come from you, both the wish and the excuse. Such sentences highlight the fact that you yourself are blocking your way. The strength of your desires is not held back by anyone other than you. You can either make excuses or earn money but not both. Successful people have the same "I would like to ... but ..." thoughts, but they trust that the first half, the wish, is stronger.

Our advice for simplification: Articulate your desires in a different way. Say, "I would like ..., and I'll achieve that by doing ...."

Money Is Reality

Some people are concerned that money will become too important in their lives. They worry that it will become a god. After all, it's not just the Bible that warns us against the "mammon of unright-eousness." Although these warnings have some justification, in everyday life they lead to a hidden devaluation of money, as is shown in the expression, "He's just doing it for the money," which is a very negative judgment. However, people who reject money inwardly will make it difficult for themselves to earn money and keep it.

In the Middle Ages there was an interesting teaching about the four elements. Gold and money belonged to the earth element—the dullest element, heavy and cumbersome. But it's only here that financial wealth is created, because action and reality also belong to the earth element.

This primitive understanding might help you to understand the subject of money. You may wish for money, want money, or have ideas about earning it, but you bring money into your account only through action. The most brilliant ideas and the strongest will won't make you rich if they're not followed up by persistent, hard, heavy work that is "down to earth" and sometimes even boring.

This is a daily experience for artists in particular: the painter is praised for his ideas, the writer for his wit, the athlete for his iron will. Consequently, we can get the impression that thought, idea, or will alone is enough to make us rich. But material success comes only when the painter actually paints a picture, the writer works consistently on his manuscript, and the athlete trains every day.

Since money is connected with earth and reality, it is a gauge that shows how rooted you are in reality. It is a good barometer for how "grounded" your life is. The life coach and banker, Hajo Banzhaf, sums it up when he says that money problems are reality problems. The word "money" could be replaced by the term "reality" in many statements. "I had such good ideas but I just didn't have the money" means "I just wasn't connected with reality." "I would be content if only I had enough money" means "I would be content if only I could accept reality."

Even the critical statement we saw at the beginning of this section ("He's just doing it for the money") doesn't sound at all so negative if we reformulate it: "He's wholeheartedly focused on reality." This is why money is a very good remedy for spiritual and artistic people. They gain inner clarity if they can move from a negative view of money to a genuine understanding of how much money their work is worth.

Simplifying Idea 6: Break the Money Spell

Becoming financially independent means having enough money so that it seldom has to become the main subject in your life. You achieve that when your income is significantly higher than your needs. The advice for simplification is therefore to either reduce your needs or increase your income. The following simplification steps are based on this fundamental idea.

Too Many Possessions Block Your Money Flow

You have spent a lot of money to acquire things. You would like to keep the things in order to feel rich through ownership and you are afraid of losses. However, this fear robs you of the opportunity of getting more. A particular characteristic of unnecessary ballast is that it increases and negative compound interest accrues. Money spent on things that do not generate more money is dead. The vital circulation of money is broken. That's why the clearing-out actions described in Step 1 are also important for improving your financial situation.

Recognition Makes You Rich

A lot of people think that you feel rich when you own a lot. But we

become truly rich through the recognition of others around us. So commit to people, not things. The most important things in life cannot be bought with money: your partner, your children, your family. The things you can buy with money must not take your attention away from people.

Money Means Using Opportunities

The next step to real wealth is the motto: fewer things, more money. That way you invest in the future, not the present. Money that is in circulation has an opportunity to increase, irrespective of whether it is in stocks, real estate, or your own company. Even if you keep what you earn in a shoebox without accumulating any interest, money means opportunities. Things, on the other hand, mean a decision that you have already made and an end to your freedom of choice.

Think of money as something in circulation that has to flow. As soon as you are worried and so you don't spend any more money and think only of yourself, you stop the flow. A society in which people hoard money will remain impoverished. A society in which everyone puts money into circulation keeps the flow going and everyone is connected with everyone else.

Many self-employed people experience this in phases. When income stops, they economize. They have fewer contacts and their reluctance communicates itself to the customers—a vicious circle. In times of crisis, it would be better to invest in advertising, networking, and PR. When money is tight, there is also a temptation to accept any contract out of desperation. But then people lose the bigger picture of the really lucrative long-term per-spectives.

Simplifying Idea 7: Get Rid of Your Debts

The basic feeling, "My life is so complicated!" often comes from a habit-ually overdrawn account. Long-term debts from consumer spending (i.e., debts for purchases that are not mortgages on property) are just like disorder in money matters. It begins with a small overdraft and then it grows continuously into bigger debt.

Oliver E. is a successful journalist. He works day and night, even week-ends, and when he's on vacation. As a freelancer, Oliver earns so much that he is envied by a lot of his colleagues. "You must be rolling in it," they tell him. But it isn't true. Oliver is always in the red and he works relentlessly against a mountain of debt that is pretty much always around the $25,000 mark. He accepts every assignment, and his body is showing the symptoms of stress: backache, obesity, susceptibility to allergies and colds. He would love to have more time for himself, but how?

Reduce the Debt Stress

Oliver E. is a typical example of a victim of the "inner account balance." This is a phenomenon that Hajo Banzhaf found in approximately 80% of people. This inner balance is usually identical with the credit line at the bank: people who are granted $25,000 overdraft protection often carry debts on that scale around with them. The unconscious mind heads for the point you're able to get to. People who are not allowed to overdraw don't overdraw and, on the whole, they make ends meet with the money they've got.

Set Up a Minimum Balance

The simplifying solution: set your "inner account balance" to a positive amount. On the box file in which you keep your bank statement, write in capital letters "MINIMUM BALANCE AT LEAST $2,500." Make sure that your account balance never falls below this level. This is good for your state of mind and it doesn't cost much. Your bank will think you're mad because you will be giving up your potential interest. The bank would think it better that you invest your $2,500 in a savings account at a measly 3% rate of interest and earn $75 per year while you're in the red at the bank paying them 18% interest for your over-draft. Resist the temptation to do this and make sure you have a reserve in your checking account and your wallet.

The Magic Dough

Money is not just a means of exchange or payment. It's a mythic meas-ure that influences more than our economic life. An account that is over-drawn for months or even years causes stress, conscious or unconscious. On the other hand, an account with a healthy balance or a wallet full of cash gives you a sense of well-being. So what is the connection? Are we automatically happier if we have lots of money in our account?

Money advisor Ralph Tegtmeier analyzed his clients and came to the astonishing conclusion that it's usually the other way around: unhappy people instinctively look for a negative value on their account. Your unconscious mind and '"invisible" worries, doubts, and fears are highlighted in this way—as minus figures on your account. Your inner mind unconsciously controls whether your bank statements show debit or credit.

According to Tegtmeier, money is a direct external manifestation of internal mental processes. You need to recognize them and come to grips with them. Then the external reality will adapt to your inner vision.

For Oliver E., the insight into this connection was virtually the solution. He was able to express his fears in a discussion with a "money therapist." His worry was that he might become like his father, whose company had gone bankrupt and who then suf-fered for the rest of his life because he had to work in a lowly position as an employee. Oliver, the son, had done better and was successful in his profession. But he constantly lived so far above his means that he couldn't enjoy being comfortable and well off. He was generous and used to invite friends to posh restaurants and he treated himself to expensive suits and luxury trips. He bought an expensive condo for the sake of tax advantages. He also paid a lot of life insurance premiums because of his fears about the future.

Oliver E. also realized that he had subconsciously gained a sense of enhanced status through credit. Banks make a high credit line attractive to their customers: it's presented as an honor and as evidence of trust. Someone who runs up a debt to the tune of $25,000 unconsciously pats himself on the back and says to himself, "I'm worth $25,000 to my bank!" Unfortunately he forgets that he's going to have to pay the bank a lot of interest for this honor.

Once Oliver resolved the deep-seated reason for his ongoing over-draft, he could return to the simple truths of money matters and expose the truth about this supposed positive side effect of debts.

Ways out of the Debt Hole

Debts can do serious damage to your self-esteem. People who have debts feel guilty, ashamed, and weak—and all because of a few figures on a piece of paper! Tell yourself again and again: I am not a bad person because I have debts; I'm just someone who has handled money badly.

Any mountain of debts can be reduced, even if it seems impossible in the beginning. A lot of people who have had the strength to do this have subsequently become millionaires, because in so doing they have discovered the power of their own will. Here are the most important steps.

1. **Face the truth.** Tell others about your debts—not everyone, of course, but tell several people whom you can trust. You will see that debts are nothing out of the ordinary and you are not the only one who has some. That will help to counteract your sense of shame. Above all, tell the members of your family. Make it clear to them that, together with them, you intend to deal with your debts.

2. **Don't spend more money than you have.** It really is that simple. Sensible loans are an exception, e.g., investing in your company or

property (provided it's not overpriced). It would be ridiculous to buy a house only when you can afford to pay cash. But keep your hands off any consumer credit that doesn't relate to assets with stable prices. A trip or new furniture on credit—don't allow yourself to be seduced!

Even the popular car loan can be dangerous. Debt counselors report that a lot of unfortunate stories from debt-ridden clients began with a loan for a new car. A car loses its value rapidly. If someone buys a new car for $18,000 and is unable to pay the interest on the loan for a while, he will then have a gigantic debt of over $18,000 (i.e., the price of the new car plus interest), although the car is now worth just $10,000 and he has to sell it. The person must then settle a debt of $8,000 with nothing to show for it!

3. **Pay in cash.** Chain stores are crazy about setting up check card  devices at the checkouts. This is because customers spend twice as much on average when they don't have to lay real money down on the table. A purse is the simplest way of keeping an overview of your personal financial situation. A lot of rich people (and quite a few bankers!) firmly believe in paying cash, even if they advertise for credit cards. A full purse or wallet gives you the pleasant feeling of being rich—and you can never overdraw on it.

4. **Slaughter your piggy banks.** Do you have savings bank books, foreign currency, or other assets that you could quickly turn into ready cash? If so, put it into your checking account immediately, because that's where you pay the highest interest, which must be reduced as quickly as possible.

5. **Go through the debits on your account.** According to a consumer counseling service in Bavaria, individual customers lose as much as 800 Euro (about $900) each year from their accounts in unnecessary items: premiums for over-insured risks, erroneous contributions for associations that the customers have already left, or donations for organizations with which the customers have long ceased to be identified. (Also, by the way, lotteries and other forms of gam-

bling are a bad investment and, strictly speaking, they are just a generous donation to the state.)

Take a critical look through last year's items. Terminate ongoing commitments, preferably by registered mail.

6. **Trim down your lifestyle.** Simplify your life in a radical way. Tell yourself, "This isn't forever, but in this phase of my life, I need to reduce. Later I'll be proud of what I have achieved."

As long as you have debts, make a sport out of saving. Put off large acquisitions. Buy reasonably priced food. Stop eating in restaurants. Don't use taxis anymore. Do without luxuries. "Tighten our belts." A smaller car is an important way to save money.

7. **Don't get used to being in the red.** Free yourself *now* from spiraling debt. People who have become accustomed to debit balances on their bank statements tend to continue managing their finances in the same way without a second thought and so they never escape from the unhealthy whirlpool. The sooner you take measures to get out, the better.

8. **Don't regard your bank as an enemy.** Burying your head in the sand, not opening invoices and bank statements—none of that helps at all. With your bank advisor, work out a realistic plan for paying off your debts. Nobody is more interested in that than your bank. You shouldn't just pay a little each month; it's better to pay as much as possible.

Always ask if there's anything you haven't fully understood. The basic principle for discussions with crafty bank advisors is question, question, question! You have to understand everything to do with your credit and your accounts, right down to the last detail. If in doubt, take a knowledgeable acquaintance or a tax advisor with you.

If nothing helps, you should consider switching to another bank. But don't set your hopes too high: banks are not especially fond of heavily indebted customers. However, it may be that another bank will value your real estate or your professional possibilities more favorably than your current bank.

9. **Every dollar counts.** People who work hard usually think that it's more important to increase income than to reduce  expenses. People who know how to manage money do both! If you work a lot and make good money, don't reward yourself by excessive spending. Continue to be as critical with purchases as you were when you were less affluent—and use what you save to build up wealth.

10. **Restructure your debts.** If your long-term debts are too high, the last resort is to raise money on your property. If you have your own house or condo and you are frequently overdrawn on your account, you can take advantage of the mortgage industry, where the interest rates are always below the rates for consumer credit. You can do this even if you don't want to build anything or remodel. For example, you might raise $10,000 on your property with a fixed rate of interest of 6% for five years. That's only half as much as the interest you would pay on an overdraft at a current rate of say 11%.

    This again is something that your bank won't be exactly enthusiastic about. But you will feel better when you've done it. But careful: don't become reckless because of the increase in your checking account. The debts are still there: they're just not as costly!

11. **The two-mountain rule.** Even if you have a lot of debt, you must save in order to accumulate wealth. This sounds like utter nonsense to people in serious trouble with debt, but it is the only real way out of the pit.

    Talk to all your creditors often and negotiate the lowest possible repayments. While you slowly reduce the debt mountain with one half of your income, you gradually build up the credit mountain with the other half and you can invest it prudently so that you earn some interest. The bottom line here is not the interest earned but the positive feeling when you see something growing again after the constant feeling of going downhill. One day in the not-too-distant future, both mountains will be equal and you will be able to pay all debts off all at once.

12. **Learn from it!** Keep on being very thrifty for a while after you pay off your debts. Use the money you've earned to make a sound investment for the future. Regard your debt phase as an important learning time. The learning objective is to ensure that nothing like that ever happens again!

Debts can be a signal that you are unconsciously bound up with someone in your family history who was unjustly treated. This is where systemic psychotherapy can help, so that your unconscious mind doesn't propel you into another phase of debt.

Agree with your partner that in the future neither one of you will sign an important contract (e.g., credit, insurance, investment contracts) without first showing it to the other; mention this to the banker or insurance salesperson. That prevents you from making rash commitments. If you just say, "I'm going to think about it," the salesperson will try to persuade you. However, he or she is powerless when faced with the partner tactic.

The most effective tip for saving would be to do without a car. But that's seldom an option, and we tend to become very attached to our set of wheels. Here's a clever compromise: sell your old car in the summer and arrange for delivery of the new one so that you are without a car for two to three months. It's quite practical in the  summer, you save money, and you can live without it for a while, as an experiment. You'll be amazed by some of the alternatives: public transport, taxis, air travel, bicycles, friendly neighbors, and rented cars.

Simplifying Idea 8:
Stop Worrying About Security

Your income is not a fate, but rather a plant that you can nourish. Take a look at the way you deal with this subject, using the following principles relating to money.

Check Your Money Reflexes

Here's a little test. On a quiz show you have two choices: a) $100,000 every day for 28 days or b) 1 cent on day 1, 2 cents on day 2, 4 cents on day 3, 8 cents on day 4, etc. for 28 days. You decide!

The idea behind this test is that your behavior relating to money has been shaped decisively during your childhood. Your reflex behavior with finances that stems from your upbringing can best be improved by a simple technique: calculation.

In the example, you get the tidy sum of $2.8 million if you take a). That's immediately obvious. A lot of people make decisions using the principle that "what you've got, you've got" and so they choose this simple option. Others sense that there must be a trick and so they blindly go for b). But that gives you $2,684,354.56—about $115,000 less.

The lesson from the example is that there isn't a spontaneous answer. As important as feelings are in money issues, in serious cases you should rely not on your instinctive reactions, but on your pocket calculator!

Look for a New Job Once per Year

You don't actually need to have the intention of changing employers. But you should regularly take a look over the fence. Our parents drummed this lesson into us: if you have a good job, work there loyally and you'll be rewarded. But this is a piece of wisdom that has long ceased to be true. Career advisors emphasize that people who remain loyal to their employer for a whole lifetime are giving away cash. They recommend changing companies at least twice in the first half of your working life, in order to climb the ladder.

People should pursue their career with their first company only if they have been promoted exceptionally early. As a rule, every change of job is a gain in experience and income.

So in order to increase your income, here's the tip for simplification: don't get too comfortable in your chair. Read the job ads. Visit other companies. Keep your ears open. Where is there a good work environment? Where are my particular abilities in great demand? Am I too old? Apply for jobs at least every three years, as an experiment—even if you don't have the slightest desire to change your job. It strengthens your self-confidence if you know that employers elsewhere would hire you. It expands your inner horizon. It can be beneficial in wage negotiations with your current employer. And you avoid finding yourself with nothing if your current firm goes bankrupt, your department is dissolved, or they get rid of you for other reasons.

Allow Others to Remunerate You for Friendly Favors

A lot of people like to give others good advice, they help people in tidying up, they look after old people—but they dare not accept money for it. Be clear about it: if you ask for a fee, you don't devalue your work; in fact, you enhance its value. If you help a helpless person, you create an inequality: you are strong and the other person is weak. If you allow the person to pay a reasonable sum of money, the inequality is reduced. That's good for both sides.

Do both: give help for money and do some things without payment. Never say, "I don't accept money on principle." That way you don't have to offend people who are generous and like to give.

If you are self-employed in a service profession, you will often be asked to reduce or even waive your fee "for a good cause." If you are tempted to respond magnanimously to all these requests, you should reconcile yourself to a definite percentage: "I'll donate 5% (or 7% or

10%) of my work to causes and organizations in which I really believe."
If you have already reached your annual figure in September, you can
refuse requests with a good conscience and good arguments.

Dare to Ask for More Money

Freelance workers normally get paid at a set rate. Such "set fees" often
do justice to their name: they remain set for years, even decades. They
 don't benefit from general increases in income.
Even with an extremely low annual rate of
increase of 2%, a fee of $250 would rise to
just over $300 in 10 years. At a modest 4%,
even after just five years, your $250 fee
would have to rise to slightly above $300 to keep pace with the increase
in the cost of living.

You just need courage here: explain to your client why your level
of remuneration is inappropriate. Present your argument objectively: if
you are still getting orders after several years, your clients are obviously satisfied with you. Don't threaten to stop, but don't be afraid of that
possibility either. Tell yourself, "Everything is going up in price and
my clients know that too. That's why they'll accommodate me when
I'm asking."

The same applies to employees. If you can prove that your work can
increase the company's profit, you should have a reasonable share in the
result.

Dos and Don'ts for Your Career

The first step to professional success is to actually want it. A lot of people don't progress in their jobs because they have unconscious blocks
against the idea of a career. Rather like the subject of money, these blocks
are associated with a whole bundle of prejudices and half-truths.

"Only kiss-ups get promoted." "You can climb the ladder only by
treading on others." "Whoever has more responsibility has to work
much more." "People in higher positions are avoided or harassed by
their former colleagues." "People who are higher up have further to

fall." These views may have a grain of truth in them, but the overall message is nonsense.

Drop these prejudices. Replace the those old sayings with new ones. After all, there are good reasons for not staying in one job for your whole life. Higher positions pay better. In a higher position, you have more scope for decision-making. People at the top are held in high esteem and they're treated better (even by their own children and spouses). Promotion brings more variety and job satisfaction. It makes it easier to move to other, more attractive companies.

The way of simplification goes (as it so often does) from the external to the internal. When it comes to careers, this is the simplification motto: if you want to have success, act like a successful person. Here are some typical situations from everyday working life and some right and wrong reactions to them.

A Colleague Is Promoted Above You

Until recently, you worked together in the same office, but now your former colleague is your superior.

Loser's attitude: You start to "work by the rules" and sabotage your former colleague. In this way, you convince your boss that he or she has promoted the right person and that you are evidently not suitable for a higher position.

Winner's attitude: Analyze (after the initial shock) what your colleague did right. Ask your boss quite frankly what you need to do to have a chance next time.

Your Boss Demands Constant Overtime

You know that people never get promoted with a time-clock mentality. But do you have to keep working an 11-hour manager's day for your measly salary?

Loser's attitude: To avoid arguments, you invent excuses to keep your evenings free. You encourage colleagues to be subversive. Or you allow yourself to be exploited under duress.

Winner's attitude: Don't say no too often. Regard your boss as your most  important customer and decide that the business relationship with him or her really matters to you. If your boss can rely on your total commitment in times of stress, you should ask for a day off or other benefit in less hectic times. If you show commitment but also have the guts to assert your own interests, your boss will have confidence that you will be able to take care of the company's interests in a higher position.

Your Budget Is Cut

Wherever you look, people are trying to save on costs. In principle, that's better than for your company to run up debts, but when your project gets cut, you might start thinking that someone is deliberately firing a shot across your bow.

Loser's attitude: You try to get funding in some other way by going over your boss's head. You do less work as a protest. You moan.

Winner's attitude: Find alternatives. If, for example, your travel budget has been cut, make as many contacts as you can on the Internet or using circulars. Look for new sources of money: grants, sponsors, new customers. Look at a budget cut as a challenge that gives you the opportunity to demonstrate your abilities to your boss. But say quite clearly that there are limits. Don't just put up with everything. Perhaps your boss is just testing to see how far he or she can go.

Your Boss Demolishes Your Suggestions in Front of the Whole Team

That hurts! It's little consolation that it's just part of life as an employee.

Loser's attitude: You retaliate in front of everyone. Or you sulk for the rest of the meeting. Or you complain about the unfair treatment to anyone who will listen.

Winner's attitude: Separate your ego from your ideas and suggestions. If your boss rejects your proposals, that's a long way from rejecting you as a person. If you found his or her style personally insulting, tell your boss in private: "I understand your decision, but I could deal with it better if you had declined my suggestions in a less personal way." Mark Wössner, former CEO of Bertelsmann, always said that he wanted to know if he had hurt a member of staff. You should also, however, pay attention in the future to the way you make suggestions. Could the boss take them as a criticism?

The Salary Increase You Wanted Is Refused

You have worked hard in a difficult year—but you don't see the fruits of it on your paycheck.

Loser's attitude: You plunder the storeroom, make more private phone calls, and leave for home punctually at the end of the day. Careful! This is playing with dynamite. If you go too far, you'll get a warning and then you'll be fired.

Winner's attitude: Ask your boss (as calmly as possible) for his or her reasons. Make suggestions for increasing revenues or saving on expenditures in such a way that you can be financially rewarded for the result. The basic rule is that you show understanding for the boss's position and present solutions to the problem. Don't forget that nobody gets a raise for one good piece of work. The most you'll get for that is a bonus. You'll get a higher salary when you offer the company added value *in the future.* Use the future in your arguments, not expectations of gratitude for the past.

You Get a New Boss

And the chemistry isn't good. He or she regards you as an enemy, and you worry that you'll soon be out of the department, together with the old office furniture.

Loser's attitude: You obfuscate and keep your knowledge to yourself. You put up blocks, act stubbornly, and refuse to cooperate.

Winner's attitude: Don't read too much into it if the new boss doesn't seem as friendly as the old one. Don't wait until the new boss calls you; take the initiative and introduce yourself. Explain your area of work  and take an interest in his or her future plans. Make yourself indispensable, but in a nice way. If you do notice that the new boss has brought in a colleague whom he or she knows well and values and wants to give the colleague your job, then you need to look around for a new position, either within the company or elsewhere. It will be easier to find it while you're still employed.

They Give You a Useless Task

In every company there are not just the great challenges but also the  "nonsense jobs" that are passed around. People see it like the old maid in the card game. And now you've got it.

Loser's attitude: You pass the old maid on or you put off coming to grips with the unpopular project.

Winner's attitude: Explain why the whole thing is unrewarding, not just for you but for the company. Even if you can't get rid of the task that way, you earn points by saying it. Good managers want to hear warnings about impending failures. In the long run, managers value staff who tell them the truth. If this isn't the case, your boss is not good enough for *you*!

Form a Goals Club

Meet every two months or so with two or three or four close friends who all want to help each other achieve success. Have a set procedure for each meeting, which may take place over lunch or dinner: you explain to each other what each of you would like to achieve in his or her occupation by the next meeting. Nobody can be successful without goals and monitoring progress toward them. Corporate climber clubs are the norm in higher management circles.

Establish Your Daily Hour for Focusing on the Future

The American life coach and best-selling author, Richard Carlson, has tested it out with many clients: people who set aside *one hour every day* for the question "How can I earn more money?" achieve financial independence after two years of consistent application of this one-hour method.

But you really need to devote a full hour *every day exclusively* to this task *without interruptions*. Most people don't achieve their financial ambitions because they throw in the towel too soon.

Approach your great future without fear or tension. Examine yourself and your abilities every day for one hour. "What do I like doing? What am I particularly good at? What skills would I like to improve further?" Be open to all the possibilities: further training, a new employer, a new occupation, a second job, or even self-employment.

Read magazines and books during this hour, watch films, phone friends and colleagues, read job ads, and keep your ears open. Give yourself some further education with courses on cassettes, videos, or books, or just take a walk for an hour and fantasize about your future.

This is important: don't drift away from the focus of your hour. Don't spend the time brooding over your past failures or present difficulties. Devote yourself to things that you don't *yet* have but could have.

If you are unemployed, visualize yourself among those who are no longer unemployed. If you are in debt, imagine yourself among people who are free from debt. If you are living on an average wage, picture yourself as one of the higher earners.

A lot of people who hear about this one-hour method laugh about the idea at first. It's difficult to see oneself as someone else. But we all live by this process—we trust that we can achieve something that exceeds our present capabilities. As a small child you learned to write. At the age of six you knew that your scribbling would one day develop into real handwriting. This is also what happens when you learn to play a musical instrument, to swim, or to ski.

The Gradual Approach to Setting up Your Own Company

A simpler and happier life .... For many people this goal is associated with the dream of no longer being an employee, of no longer having your schedule dictated by others, of no longer being demotivated by incompetent superiors, of determining your own income. For many people, this remains no more than a dream, because they don't trust themselves to stand on their own two feet. And yet it's easier than they think.

Even if self-employment is an idea that you emphatically reject at first, just try thinking about it. Even as an employee, you should be able to imagine what it's like to be self-employed. There is a distinct trend in business toward profit center organization and, in the most developed companies, every employee has long been regarded as a mini profit center and partner. Here are the necessary simplification steps.

Warm up. You don't have to jump into self-employment. While you're working as an employee, build up a second base. Test yourself in the market. Get into a hobby on a semi-professional basis. What do you really enjoy doing? What makes your heart leap? That's the best place to begin. Don't think primarily about money and where you could most easily earn it. Otherwise, you'll land on the old treadmill again and just work for the income—and not for your personal fulfillment.

Find an advisor. It doesn't have to be an expensive business consultant; in the beginning, your tax advisor will do. He or she will initiate you into the secrets of the tax return and sales and use taxes, the first two subjects to learn about on your way to self-employment. You'll soon see that it's all easier than you feared.

A critical factor on your way to becoming self-employed is to know someone else who's done it, someone whom you value and with whom you can talk. Without a living example, it's almost impossible to move into a new livelihood.

Set high goals for yourself. Motivational trainers emphasize that goals are never too high; there are just time periods that are too short. Most people overestimate what they can achieve in two months—but they underestimate what is possible in two years. Never make mediocrity your goal. Don't be just one of many; become number one in your clearly defined field!

Don't sell products. Sell solutions. According to entrepreneur Jörg Knoblauch, the first rule in business is that you sell a benefit. A good car dealer doesn't go about selling cars; he sells a life experience. A PC shop doesn't sell computers; it sells labor-saving advantages. Express the aim of your future business in an active, customer-focused form. "I'm going to create value for my customers ...." Your objective should not be to maximize profit, but rather the tangible benefits of your product or service. That's the only way to get the profit you're looking for.

Stand by your name. The best name for your business is not something fanciful (MegaTurboSysTec) but your actual name (John Smith Tennis Club). This is because wherever you appear, whenever your name is mentioned, there is, in effect, advertising for your company (even if you are a one-person business). Moreover, nothing gives customers more confidence than a flesh-and-blood person.

Don't run your competitors down. Be convincing with your own product or service. Learn from your competitors' strengths and avoid their mistakes. Don't be discouraged by the fact that there are other providers out there. There are enough customers for everyone! But don't ever make your competitors' weaknesses the focus when you advertise or solicit customers. Formulate what you have to offer in such a way that it sounds unique

and your customers don't even think of comparing you with your competitors.

Set reasonable prices. Never get involved in giveaway offers or introductory prices. Offer something of better value than the competition and make it clear that this is what you are doing. Establish yourself in the lucrative upper segment of the market where quality alone is the decisive factor. If the quality of your work is outstanding, the price argument will take second place.

Believe in yourself. You are always only as good as you think you are.
 Speak well of yourself without boasting or exaggerating. Create your own advertising material. Be bold enough to use superlatives: "the friendliest office service in the area," "the smallest wholesaler in the country," "the most creative Internet designer you can get for the price."

Stick to it. Don't be discouraged by failure. On the contrary, all successful people have discovered and developed their real strengths through failures. Walt Disney was turned down by over 300 banks—and then the 303rd bank financed his planned Disneyland. Winston Churchill, in a speech that characterized his life, said, "Never give in, never give in, never, never, never, never—in nothing, great or small, large or petty—never give in!"

Be thrifty. Increase your income with your own money by investing it intelligently. Flashy office furniture is dead capital. A sum of $25,000 invested 20 years ago in fixed-interest security funds and equity funds would be worth well over $500,000 by now.

Your company philosophy: love and passion. Never do work you don't like just for the money. If you lose your love for your (new) occupation, stop doing it. If your new job causes you to lose the affection of your life partner, stop doing it. As Americans say, "Love it or leave it."

Simplifying Idea 9:
Work Out Your Own Concept of Wealth

Once you have begun to pay off absurd debts and are well on the way to a stage where money is no longer the central focus of your life, you should finally resolve to keep it that way.

This begins in your head. Get rid of the idea that being rich has something to do with money. It is erroneous to determine poverty and wealth by figures and comparisons with other people. Any poor person will know someone who is even poorer. Every rich person knows someone who has more money. And nobody is poor simply because he or she doesn't have much money.

Wealth and poverty are matters of awareness. Sooner or later a person who is aware of his or her wealth will find that material "wealth" will come too. The quotation marks are intended to highlight the fact that a person who is aware of his or her wealth will feel rich even with relatively little money and property.

You can become rich now, i.e., right now while you're reading this book. It's very simple: you just tell yourself, "I'm rich." If you can't say that now, you won't say it in 10 years, no matter how much you have earned or lost. For most people this insight is a great relief. It means that their search is at an end.

With the following tips, you will have your material possessions under control and you will experience a new dimension of wealth.

Write Down Your Expenses

This doesn't have to turn into a form of private bookkeeping. It's not that important what you do with the lists you make. The decisive thing is that the written form makes you aware of the money you're spending. A good many silly, spontaneous purchases are prevented because  your unconscious mind thinks, "Oh dear, tomorrow I'll look at my spending list and I'll regret this nonsense!" Stay rich and at the same time modest—your awareness of wealth must not lure you into crazy extravagance.

Don't Lead Yourself into Temptation

Pay by cash where possible. There's a great temptation to pay with a card and thus lose your feeling for the amounts you are spending. Take your credit card only when you have to pay a large amount that you don't want to carry around with you in cash; when you pay, imagine the card in your hand turning into a bundle of dollar bills and then, in your imagination, pay out the amount in cash onto the checkout counter.

Donate Specific Amounts

The great psychological paradox concerning money is that if you give money to people in need, you feel rich. Giving really can lead to a reduction in spending. This is because your unconscious mind will admonish you to exercise financial restraint after making a donation; it has to do this in order to continue to feel that you are rich. Some people think they would feel richer if they didn't donate anything at all and just spent a lot on themselves: elegant clothes, grandiose vacations. But the unconscious mind gives us a hard time for such egotism and sooner or later there will be a disaster relating to the money that is coming in. You can see this if you watch the "beautiful people" carefully: they lose their wealth in reckless financial maneuvers. (Exceptions prove the rule.)

Don't just donate to organizations but also to actual people. Help someone else to achieve success. Nothing else will motivate you more powerfully to achieve your own success. There is a saying that the best way to learn is to teach.

Be guided by the principle that whoever wishes to reap riches must first sow the seeds. Many people have no real idea how to do that. But they can sow the seeds of poverty by showing low esteem. This applies especially to tips. Try this: when you check out of a hotel, leave $5 in the room for the maid and then do without something that would have cost the same amount. (For example, don't have a drink in the bar.) When you close the hotel door behind you, you will have a feeling that's priceless—the sense of being rich.

Regard an Inheritance as a Gift

No other event is so frequently likely to cause family disputes as inheritance. The squabbling frequently begins during the lifetime of the person who is expected to leave money. "OK, Susan's just looking after Uncle John so that she'll be well remembered in his will."

The good advice from Munich-based psychotherapist Jakob Schneider is to regard inherited money or other property as a gift if you have not earned it by working for it. Only then can you forgo your share with a sense of integrity if disputes arise. The others who are "greedy" will often not be so obsessed with the share that is due to you and it will be easier to come to a compromise. It is often good, when there's a dispute, to waive your right to part of your inheritance; peace can then return to the situation. If you waive your right to the inheritance entirely and others think you are trying to hold yourself up as a great exemplar of virtue, the relationship with the one who gets everything will be difficult or it may even be permanently ruined.

Always Be Fair in Your Financial Transactions

A remarkable but not very well-known comment by Christ on the subject of money is "Make to yourselves friends of the Mammon of unrighteousness." He says this with a very long-term view: if there is no money (in the next life), it won't be the balance sheet that counts but rather the good deeds that you have done with the money.

This does not apply just to your own money but also to resources

71

that you manage for other people. Some employees think it's in their employer's best interests to push suppliers to the absolute limit and to squeeze as much money as possible out of customers. However, it's better for you (and for your company in the long run) to pay more attention to the relationship with people than to the numbers alone. Make friends by treating people fairly in financial matters. A little generosity in the right place can do wonders for your relationship with a tradesperson, supplier, or service provider.

You sow the seeds of poverty if you don't settle invoices or you make people wait a long time for payment. People who don't give others what is due to them will find sooner or later that they don't get what is due to them. Just think: someone who doesn't pay a bill doesn't stand sovereign over the filthy lucre, but rather clings to every penny until he or she receives the third reminder letter. Neurotic clinging cannot make you rich. A survey in America has shown that companies that pay invoices promptly are regarded not as stupid but noble and successful.

But the seeds of poverty are also sown by people who buy things they can't afford and then can't pay the bills for them. They insult their creditors by not giving them what is due.

Wish Others Well

Don't begrudge others what they have. Wish for it to increase. Wish them good health and fortune. This applies especially to people who have more than you. It's not that difficult to sincerely wish for a beggar to be rich. But it will be much more difficult to wish for your boss or a millionaire to become richer.

Whatever you devote your attention to will grow. If a government focuses on shortages and introduces austerity measures, it gives unemployment and poverty extra energy. If a company concentrates on reducing expenditures, it will be difficult for the company to present itself to customers as attractive and forward-looking. But those who concentrate on added value and prosperity will reap prosperity.

Think Positively About Money

Even if you still have debts at the moment or you don't know how you are going to earn a living soon, don't fall into condemning money and prosperity. Don't develop hate or envy toward people who have enough. What you think will become a reality for you: if you hate wealth and money, then these things won't come your way. Someone who hates money will also be thinking negatively about himself and his capacity for work. He won't have any confidence in himself and he won't earn money—the cycle is complete.

Get this straight. Your work is what you think of it. Your customers are what you think of them. The economic situation is what you think of it.

Think of the World as an Abundance

The basic principle of nature is abundance. Millions of sperm are produced, even though just one is used. The universe is immeasurably large and it has existed for an inconceivably long time. Have faith that there is enough for everyone. Of course it's not possible for everyone on the planet to become a multimillionaire. But don't regard a rich person as someone who is taking something away from you. See that person as a potential good customer or contributor. Regard yourself as someone who can share in the abundance of creation.

You Decide Your Financial Reality

It will sometimes seem to you as though everyone is conspiring against you, as though life is against you. But that just cannot be the case. Life is simply life. The only reason that life seems to be against you lies in *your* thinking about life. And the way you think has a greater effect on your reality than you would ever dream possible. People who suffer from a persecution complex see underground gangs with spies and informers. They are absolutely convinced, even when all the facts point in the opposite direction.

It works in a similar way with financial matters. Sometimes it may seem to you as if money goes everywhere but just not your way. As soon as you are convinced of this, it actually will not come to you any more. Your unconscious will cause you to behave with a career-damaging attitude at work and to invest your money unwisely, etc.

Regard yourself as a performer in life and not as a victim. Always keep your sense of humor, like the actress Mae West, who made a clear statement about money: "I've been rich and I've been poor. Believe me, rich is better."

Become Rich by Saving

Try toying with this thought: wouldn't it be a simple life if you could live on the interest on your savings and do a job that you like and that makes you really happy? If you could devote all your energy to other people—without worries about money?

Save a specific amount at the beginning of the month. This advice is the basic idea of money advisor Bodo Schäfer. He recommends replacing the word "save" with the expression "pay yourself." Have a set amount transferred from your account at the beginning of every month. This is the only way to be certain that you don't use the money for something else. People who save "whatever's left at the end of the month" generally have an empty account.

Take advantage of compound interest. With a clever way of saving, you can marvel at the wonder of the effect of compound interest on your own account. If you put away $500 each month and find an investment with a 12% rate of return (this has been the case with almost all good equity funds over the past few decades), after 21 years you will have $500,000. This asset then can give you a monthly income of $5,000—without having to touch the capital. The figures might look embellished, but in recent years they were even better! Even if individual crises shake the economy, it's a good strategy to build up wealth with stock. In the United States, almost all old-age pensions are based on this strategy. Large sums will continue to flow into the economy and keep it running.

After the enormous falls from 2000 to 2002, there has been a gradual upward trend in stock prices, albeit not as dramatic as in the boom years 1997 to early 2000.

Clearing up in the money level of your life pyramid can bring about a small miracle. As we have already stressed, money is more than just a means of payment. Your relationship with money is an important aspect of your personality and an important step toward a simple and happy life. We now come to an aspect that is even closer to you: the way you manage your time.

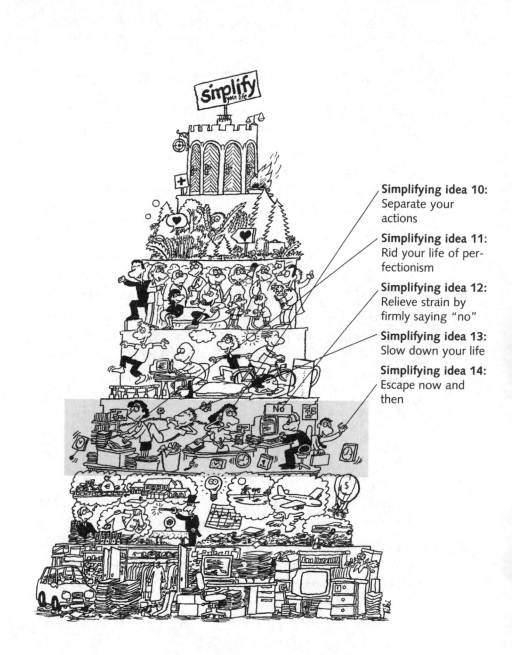

Simplifying idea 10:
Separate your actions

Simplifying idea 11:
Rid your life of perfectionism

Simplifying idea 12:
Relieve strain by firmly saying "no"

Simplifying idea 13:
Slow down your life

Simplifying idea 14:
Escape now and then

Step 3 of Your Life Pyramid:
Simplify Your Time

Your Dream of Simplicity: Fourth Night

"From up here money looks quite different and things down there just look so ridiculously harmless." Such thoughts go through your head when you have found your way to the third level of your pyramid. You are now prepared to encounter feelings here again, primarily, and suddenly a thought flashes through your mind: perhaps your life pyramid consists of nothing but feelings.

But when you take a closer look at the third step, you see that this is not the case. Besides your feelings, there's an infinite range of new images to marvel at, allegories and stories from the depths of your soul. The walls of the third story consist of a strange porous material, like bone or sandstone, and you notice that you are walking on crunchy sand. A white powder is slowly trickling out of the holes in the walls. You feel the wall carefully. Actually, the sand is coming from these walls themselves, as though you are being worn away by an inner force. One day these walls won't hold up any more; they will have broken down. You become aware for the first time that this pyramid will not stand forever, but only for the length of your life.

But the walls of the third story still look very sturdy. In some places there are huge weights hanging on it, wondrous shapes and grimacing faces distorted with pain, colorful constructions and dark-gray blocks of stone. Many are moving and your feelings tell you that this is all about your activities, your tasks and duties, your hobbies and preferences. With some of them you feel oppressive weight on your shoulders, whereas with others you have a sense of lightness and joy.

You would have expected a clock to be hanging here, but then you see that there are just lots of clocks at wide intervals, like satellites circling around this third story. You understand that your life pyramid does not contain any clock hands or digital displays. You see that the measurement of time is a dimension added from outside. Even when you try to grasp for the flying clocks, you can never reach them or influence them in any way. On the other hand, you find that not only can you touch the many tasks on the wall, but you can move them effortlessly with a light push. That surprises you, because you would have expected them all to be screwed tight onto your pyramid so that they couldn't be moved. Now you sense what your task on this step will be.

Simplifying Objective for Step 3

Learn to manage
your time actively.

When we look at the subject of time, the initial situation is more clear and fair than with any other resource: every person has 24 hours each day. So why do some people have "no time" while others get bored? Because the language is misleading: when someone has "no time," the disorder is not in his or her time but in his or her tasks. There are too many things: things that are too big and things that are too unimportant that the person packs into those 24 hours. Simplification does not mean "saving time" but rather "saving tasks." It's not a question of managing time. It's a question of managing yourself.

That is the secret of the third step of your life pyramid: at one point you make a path by removing superfluous activities and making one of your many activities the most important one. Then you will have the glorious feeling of being master of your time and then you will have reached the next step in your way of simplification.

Simplifying Idea 10: Separate Your Actions

The secret of successful and happy people is usually that they are able to concentrate totally on one thing. Even if they have a lot in their head, they have found a method so that the many commitments don't impede each other; instead they are brought into a good inner order. And this order is quite simple: the most important first!

In theory, it's quite clear, but in everyday life it seems rather different. You might have tried to decide on priorities, but perhaps you failed because of everyday trivial matters and all the unforeseen distractions. Take the path of time simplification to a new era of self-management.

Absolute Simplicity

Set a clear priority for your personal and professional tasks: 1 for very important, 2 for secondary importance, and 3, 4, and so on for less important or negligible. Sometimes priorities are given by time pressure—but don't trust this. Not everything that is urgent is really important. First place is for things that have an above-average chance of being profitable, things that have a great development potential, or that a very large number of people will notice. What is new in the way of simplification is the *uncompromising simplification*. Just take on one single priority from level 1 each day.

Even if you try to take on only two tasks at once, your energy will be dissipated. Even if you deal with the second task only in your mind, you will be weakening your inner strength. The secret is in separating one priority from the next as much as possible. To do so, you should use the following two techniques.

Keep Your Life Free for the Important Things

Make clear agreements with the people who are waiting for you to complete tasks you've rated as 2, 3, or lower. Make room for priority 1. Don't take on any unrealistic deadlines; otherwise, you'll fall back into the old vicious circle.

You'll get menacing phone calls with the old refrain, "But you promised me ...." Keep calm when the other person becomes pushy and says, "What? In four weeks? I absolutely need it in four days!" Don't be intimidated. Speak the truth: it can't be done quicker. The danger of losing customers this way or endangering your job within a company is usually overestimated.

In the long run, it's much worse if you don't keep to the deadlines that you yourself have promised. The important thing is that you keep your head clear for priority number 1. That is the *principle of keeping your life clear for the important things*.

Take Action Against Disturbances

Separate off disturbances (for example, by escaping into a second office; see Simplifying Idea 14) and start the day with task number 1. Don't allow any distractions to get in the way. Put off your favorite routine tasks till later (opening the mail, surfing the Internet, watering the flowers, ordering new teddy bears ...).

Reward yourself with easy activities only when you have completed the first stage of task number 1. Just think: the beginning is always the most difficult. You have to give yourself the impetus. After a while it will be much easier. In the beginning it's a real battle and you need to take the bull by the horns. That is the *principle of the consciously focused defense*.

You will see: when you concentrate on *one* task, you find you have energy that you didn't even know you had. Just imagine: you are at a fair and you have to carry two heavy pigs over a 100-yard stretch. If you keep grabbing one and then the other, it will take forever, because one of them will keep slipping out from under your arm and running off. But if you tether one pig, pick up the other, gather all your strength and make a dash for the finish line, pause for a moment, run back and get the other one, grit your teeth with great determination, and carry the second pig to the finish line, then you can be sure of success and applause from the spectators!

Celebrate Your Successes

When you have dealt with task number 1, celebrate it! Either on your own or with others. Dance around the room, lie down on the grass or stroll through the streets, treat yourself to a beer in the evening in a corner bar or a lovely meal with your partner. Really let yourself experience the good feeling of having done something and enjoy it.

No matter how many new urgent tasks are waiting with a great big menacing 1, this is a time to just have the positive experience! You must not allow yourself to be deprived of this moment of happiness by anyone, least of all yourself! This is the important culmination of the project.

People who don't do this experience their life as a burden and their occupation as a treadmill. Try out the *principle of celebrating life*, preferably today.

Simplifying Idea 11:
Rid Your Life of Perfectionism

"If only I were slimmer, more beautiful, richer, more clever, then I would be happier." This is a dream that makes a lot of people ill, frustrated, and unhappy. This was discovered by counselors Enid Howarth and Jan Tras of Albuquerque. They both say that the ineradicable myth of the perfect life is a dangerous illusion. It ties up energy instead of providing impetus. They encourage people instead to move toward a happy and relaxed imperfection. Life has its flaws, defects, corners, and edges. Only those who accept this reality and integrate it into their existence can lead a really full life.

Of course there are activities in which errors are dangerous: driving a car, crossing the road, handling medicines. But life doesn't consist entirely of these things. In among them there is a lot of room for small and large blunders. Research at the University of New Mexico revealed that excessive meticulousness not only makes people ill but also causes economic damage. Those who find a middle way between sloppiness and perfection live a happier and simpler life and also save more money.

"Better Immediately" Principle

This principle can be illustrated nicely in an everyday situation. You notice a dust ball gathering in a corner of the room. *Reaction 1:* you sigh and say it's time to give the house a good cleaning, but you leave the dirt there because cleaning here would be like "a drop in the ocean." *Reaction 2:* you simply pick of the dust ball and throw it away.

Reaction 1 is perfectionism. Actually that would be the best solution because if there is dirt here then there will surely be dirt elsewhere. But usually the perfect action you've planned doesn't come about soon and the specific problem remains unresolved.

Reaction 2 is the simple and pragmatic solution. It has two attractive advantages: the direct problem is resolved and what you do does not keep you from doing a perfect spring-cleaning later.

Swiss business consultant Samuel Brunner impresses this goal on managers who have been groomed for total quality: "as well as necessary" and not better. Getting rid of perfectionism involves the courage to leave gaps and the courage to improvise.

People Who Make Mistakes Become Winners

A doctrine that has contributed to the development of perfectionism and that a lot of people have internalized is that "if I don't do everything completely right, I am a failure." And yet the greatest inventions are the result of a lot of failed experiments coupled with the indefatigable will of the inventor to succeed. Mistakes are an opportunity to do something better next time. Mistakes are learning experiences.

Our advice for simplification: Start to appreciate your mistakes. Watch other people: their mistakes are often the most interesting thing about  them. Say to yourself, "My mistakes make me unique and valuable." Stand in front of the mirror, look at yourself with glowing pride, and say out loud, "I stand by my mistakes." You might, for example, be able to write wonderful reports, but never on time. You might be an outstanding organizer, but you take on too much. You work on one thing with admirable tenacity, but sometimes it's something that's just not worthwhile.

Be grateful for the kindness of others who, by and large, can live with your mistakes. Accept your imperfect self. After all these years, you've earned it! The following exercises can help to break down excessive perfectionism.

The list of 14 things. If you feel like a failure, make a list of 14 things that you have done today. You made a great pot of coffee, you went down the stairs without stumbling, you drove without having an accident, you mastered word processing on your PC ….

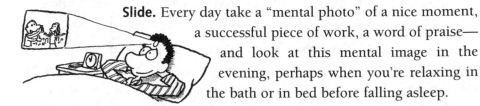

Slide. Every day take a "mental photo" of a nice moment, a successful piece of work, a word of praise—and look at this mental image in the evening, perhaps when you're relaxing in the bath or in bed before falling asleep.

Damage report. Enjoy your mistakes. Tell others about them. Make a nice story out of them. People love hearing that others have messed things up. Today's mishaps are often tomorrow's anecdotes! Try it out. You won't lose esteem: you'll gain affection.

The "blissful imperfections" day. Allow yourself moments of imperfection or even have a completely imperfect day on purpose. Wear something unsuitable. Go into the office without ironing your trousers. Ask for help. Say, "I don't know" in reply to a question. Call a wrong number and say, "Sorry!"

Such deliberately unsuccessful days relax your unconscious mind, which may be fixated on the idea that every day must be a step forward. But it doesn't have to be! Start to appreciate the calm rhythm of your heartbeat, with the normal cycle of life.

Not Everything Is Possible

"Perfection is achievable." That's a myth of modern industrial society, hammered into our unconscious minds millions of times by advertising: the perfect house, the flawless body, the complete financial plan for our golden years.

In reality, however, perfection is rare, fleeting, and usually achieved only by chance. Even supposedly perfect systems (like space vehicles, for example) don't work 100%. They just work (almost) perfectly because

all the systems are multiple, through redundancy—the designers prepare for each function to be imperfect.

Car manufacturers say that people who buy new cars want to exchange whole parts or even the whole car because of tiny scratches. Many people expect this extreme perfection from themselves as well. They carry around a merciless judge inside them. The inner voice is loudest when they get up, when they go to sleep, or immediately after they've made a mistake: "You should have done it better" or "You can do it better" or "Shame on you!"

The simplifying solution: Don't strive to be perfect, but competent and unique. Release yourself into a relaxed normality. You can more or less live with other people's faults. Be just as magnanimous with yourself. Turn down the volume of your inner judge. Tell your inner voice, "I can hear you; you don't need to shout."

Try to imagine your judge as a real person. Draw a sketch, shape a clay figure, or do a collage with magazine pictures. Look at your judge and see how cruel and ugly he or she is. Then give your judge the place he or she deserves: put the image in a box of old things or give it a place in the doghouse. You cannot kill or gag your internal judge. But you can show your judge that he or she is not the boss of your life.

Make up an amusing sentence to describe yourself. Here are a few suggestions: "I am capable, likeable, clever, and I'm imperfect through and through." "The stages of development in my life: perfect, past perfect, imperfect." "I am imperfect and I succeed at being imperfect without even having to try." "My mistakes are better than yours." "I'm imperfect—that's how I am."

You Are Worth More than What You Do

"You are what you achieve" is the creed of a lot of trainers—a dangerous half-truth. Of course people who are active and work on themselves  have more weight in the personal and social sense than people who just suffer life passively. But when people define themselves only by what they do, they give themselves and others no room to enjoy their personality. All along the edge of the path of simplification, you will keep seeing big signs that say, "You are worth more than your activities!"

If work takes up all of your life, there isn't any balance. Use the following test to see whether you are too far removed from your life balance in this respect. You will be happy only when you can devote yourself appropriately to all the areas of your life.

Test

Check off any statements that apply to you:

❏ I am always busy.

❏ I sometimes do more than is humanly possible.

❏ Boredom: I don't know what that is.

- ❏ Exhaustion lifts my mood.
- ❏ My schedule is so tight that I can't ever allow anything to go wrong.
- ❏ I often have pain in my neck, shoulders, or back.
- ❏ I am often amazed at how quickly I do certain tasks.
- ❏ I love the feeling of being financially not just secure but exceptionally secure.

If you've checked off more than one statement, you might be buying into the "American dream" about what you can do: aim high, strive with dogged determination, make more money.

The simplifying solution: In the way you arrange your life, include your body, your relationships with other people, and the search for meaning in your life, together with pleasure and the urge to work and achieve. Break your own strict rules now and then. Do something ecstatic. Consciously take time for things that don't generate any money or success but that are just fun. Listen to your family, your friends, and your body and fulfill their wishes.

Lower Your Stress Limit

"I can handle stress" is regarded as a positive statement in the world of work. People who can deal with a lot of pressure and remain calm under great stress are seen as exemplary. Most books and seminars on stress management teach methods of raising the stress limit. The way of simplification goes in the opposite direction: stand by your weaknesses.

There is a sort of natural law in psychology just as in physics: the level of stress to which you are exposed corresponds exactly to your capacity to cope with it. People who can handle stress (and openly declare it) are given more and more to cope with—until one day they break.

Pay careful attention to the signs that tell you that you are under more stress than you can cope with. These signals can come from various areas of life, so you might not recognize the connection at first. You become ill (problems with your heart, stomach, or back). Or your work performance decreases, you become the victim of harassment and mobbing (collective psychological and emotional abuse). Or your relationship runs into trouble, divorce seems likely, the children rebel. Or your general mood becomes depressive; you look for an escape in alcohol, drugs, or an addictive hobby.

Allow Yourself to Be Weak

If you have any of these symptoms, change your life agenda and decrease your tolerance of stress. Say quite openly, "I can't manage that." Even though you could do it if necessary, by summoning up all your reserves, as you have done in the past. Talk about your problems quite openly and look for helpers and allies. Allow yourself time out, like people do when they're ill. If absolutely necessary, steal time for yourself. Leave the office earlier. Take a stroll on the way home from work. Find time to be alone and get some distance from work stresses *and* private difficulties.

Don't keep on doing everything people expect of you. Simply stop functioning. You will see that the consequences are less serious than you feared. In fact, your spouse or partner will even find you so much more lovable. When you're free from pressure, you will breathe a sigh of relief and sense that you have come one step nearer to the essentials of life—not through your strengths but through your weaknesses.

Simplify Old Procedures

In any company or organization, there are long-established procedures that nobody really questions anymore. And woe to anyone who does. "That's how we've always done it" is frequently the reply. Your response should be the key question in any forward-looking company: "How can we do it more simply?" Let's look at a few examples.

Immediate List Instead of Minutes

It is incredible how many meetings are still held in which the person taking the minutes then has to type up those handwritten notes on a PC and send them to all the participants. There are flowery phrases like "The chair emphasized the fact that ...." In the really crusty old structures, there is even the agenda item "Approval of previous minutes." And it's not just that taking the minutes is one of the worst jobs to be given. This method wastes working capacity. It takes time to take the minutes in this way and it really has a place only in parliamentary meetings.

Our advice for simplification: During the meeting, the person responsible for taking the minutes writes down a list of the most important results in reasonably legible handwriting. The structure of each result is relatively simple: who does what by when? At the end of the meeting, the person reads out his or her notes (this replaces the laborious "approval of previous minutes") and then makes copies of them and gives a copy to each participant. At the next meeting, this "immediate list" is used to check whether all tasks have been completed.

Direct Connect Instead of Through Organization Operators

Many times a letterhead just includes the main number of the organization. This can be a sign of ineffectiveness. If all callers have to go through one contact point, the price is irritation and working time, both for callers and staff. Phone systems save staff time and energy, but can still take a toll on callers.

The simplification method: Put your extension number in big, clear print on all your letters. If you work somewhere else from time to time, redirect any calls. Statistically speaking, that's more effective than having the switchboard or receptionist locate you: the person requested is found in only 20% of all cases. If you cannot be contacted, use your voice mail or switch the calls to an answering machine. That's more practical than letting somebody take a message. Also, reduce general telephone inquiries, for example by including in a brochure or catalogue extension numbers for the relevant contact people for individual products.

A Pool of Experts Instead of an Advisory Committee or Other Meeting

A company is as impressive as the illustrious names of the members of its various advisory committees. They are convened regularly, which costs time and money for all those involved. Some dignitaries make valuable suggestions while others just slurp their coffee. This also applies to honorary bodies, church councils, or club committees. A general rule: meetings are held much too regularly.

The simplification method: Invite to an initial in-depth meeting experts who can help you, so they can get to know your company and its employees. From then on, contact should not be through regular meet-

ings but directly between the individuals with responsibility in the company and the advisors with the relevant competence. That may be by phone, e-mail, fax, or personal meetings. Only those advisors who genuinely can help should be consulted. That's better for both parties. The illustrious names of committee members can appear on letterhead or brochures with a better conscience, now that they are really doing what they were recruited for—giving advice.

Flat-Rate Payments Instead of Travel Expense Reports

Hardly any subject is so explosive or causes such consternation as expense reports for business trips. Accountants suspect that the people who travel have fun and get rich on the expenses while the people who travel feel doubly punished: they're away from their families and they're out of pocket temporarily.

The simplification method: Arrange flat-rate payments for business trips that occur frequently, based on the rates paid so far. That saves time-consuming calculations on the part of the travelers and the accountants. The person who takes a trip is motivated to stay in a reasonably priced hotel or to take a bus to the airport instead of a taxi, because he or she pockets the money saved (although it's taxable as income). As long as the flat-rate payments remain within bounds and don't create the impression of a additional salary in disguise, the company should not incur any tax disadvantages. Travel expenses are business expenses for a company, whether they are based on internal flat rates or tax-rate tables.

A Bulletin Board Instead of Routing or E-Mail

Messages intended for everyone ("parking lot closed tomorrow due to construction") are sometimes conveyed through documents that are routed around or often by e-mail. The documents often get stuck with one person and e-mails tend to be overlooked.

Our advice for simplification: Innovative companies stand out by their well-arranged bulletin boards located where all staff members walk past them. Current messages are posted on a particularly prominent board; they are quickly identified as new by a symbol or varying colors. Don't be dissuaded by people who say, "Nobody looks at that." After a brief time for acclimation, people take it for granted that they should look at the board every day—provided that notices are removed as soon as they become obsolete.

Walking Instead of a Meeting

Conferences take place in conference rooms with a lot of unhealthy rituals: coffee, donuts, sitting still around the table. In the worst cases, the room is filled with smoke because the smokers have the upper hand.

The simplification method: Try holding a discussion outside. If there are no more than five people, you can even hold discussions while walking. Socrates used to walk around with his disciples during his seminars and used to get his best ideas that way.

Expand Your Time Horizon

You have an appointment calendar, perhaps even a schedule planner or a PDA. You prepare to-do lists. You plan particular activities for each day. But there is always something else. Something always comes up. At the end of the day, you're facing a mountain of tasks that you still have to deal with. Time management, actually intended to facilitate a relaxed and happy life, all too often becomes a source of tension and unhappiness.

Do yourself a favor and rethink it. Turn time planning back into a real tool that is under your control. Don't tell yourself anymore, "I have to deal with this important task today." Instead say, "I need to find a good day for this important task."

The difference is that you're not reacting then to what the appointment calendar says; you're acting freely. You're moving from reaction to action. You're not pinned down by the appointment, but rather, you're pinning down the appointment.

Plan on a Weekly Basis

In practice, active time management works best if you stop integrating the to-do list into your daily schedule but instead uncouple the two. There are special, loose to-do sheets for most time planning systems.

They can be pulled out so that you can look at the list of important tasks next to your schedule. In electronic time planners, the to-do lists are normally organized independently anyway. Now you decide which tasks you're going to take on today. You *actively* give priority to one of your to-do items. You are the boss, not your calendar!

This is only a small difference in terms of the way you work, but it may mean a revolution for you in matters of time management. In the beginning, put as much on the foldout to-do list as you can manage in one week. But don't be discouraged if tasks have to be incorporated into the following week. You are the master of your time!

It's good to cross the completed items off the list in a ceremonial way and enjoy the feeling of having completed something.

Set Yourself Big Goals

When you have assimilated the new way of working and relating to things, you can put larger projects and visions on the to-do list and connect them with the activities of the particular day. That way you constantly have your eye on the big projects and goals. There's no longer a danger of drowning in the trivial tasks of everyday life. Just think: small goals, small successes—big goals, big successes!

If you continue to do what you're doing currently, you will never achieve more than you're achieving at the moment.

Simplifying Idea 12:
Relieve Strain by Firmly Saying "No"

If you have the feeling that 24 hours per day are not enough for all the things you need to do, then it's not because the day has too few hours, but because you have too many activities. A simple fact that overloaded people often tend to forget. The simplifying solution is equally simple: don't accept so many work assignments in your private life or your working life. People who work without resting become ill.

The pressure at work is on the increase in all occupations and in all sectors. Employees worry about keeping their jobs and self-employed people are concerned about losing customers. The strain in the interpersonal realm is also increasing. In the modern nuclear family, the expectations that formerly would have been shared among all the relatives are now concentrated on the individual partner.

No. Unfortunately I can't come due to the following reasons ...

What is the result? Employees allow themselves to get saddled with too many commitments and the self-employed accept too many contracts. The family is on edge as a result of excessive overtime work. To keep the peace at home, those who are already under too much pressure agree to take on more than they can really manage in their private lives. They grit their teeth and say "Yes" because they are afraid of the consequences of saying "No." The art of simplification consists of being firm in simply saying "No."

Healthy Self-Awareness Makes It Possible to Say "No"

Manuel J. Smith, a professor of psychology in Los Angeles, has specialized in this problem. His theory is that when people say "Yes" although they really mean "No," it isn't primarily about them but about being *manipulated* by someone else.

His therapy consists of increasing their awareness. When you get into a yes-no situation, say the following sentence to yourself: "I have a right not to be manipulated by others—not by my boss, not by my clients, not even by my partner, not by my relatives, not by my best friend."

In such a situation, stand as upright as possible, with both feet flat on the ground, hold your back straight, and calmly say to yourself, "I am me and I have my space, which belongs to me and no one else."

The positive concept to counter attempts at manipulation is your *right to self-determination*—and this is a basic requirement for your healthy participation in human relationships. This right to self-determination can be summarized in the following five points.

1. **Emotional sovereignty.** You have the right to evaluate your own feelings. For example, your boss says, "Go and see Mr. Smith and persuade him to apply for the position." You say, "Someone else will have to do it. I can't stand the man. I can't do it." Your boss says, "Nonsense, you'll manage it." The sentence sounds encouraging, but it amounts to manipulation: he's dismissing your feelings. You have the right to your feelings and to be respected by other people. So you need to say, "That would be impossible for me. Send someone else. That will be better for all concerned!"

2. **Sovereignty in matters of taste.** You have the right not to have to make excuses for your preferences. A saleswoman asks you, for example, "Why don't you like the coat?" You say, "I don't like the color." She says, "This color is in fashion. All our customers like it." Don't let yourself be drawn into any further discussion. As soon as you begin to justify your taste or make excuses for it, you weaken your self-esteem and make it possible for the other person to manipulate you.

3. **Sovereignty of judgment.** If you are to solve other people's problems, you have the right to assess the problems. Your spouse might say, "Go and pick up my aunt from the airport tomorrow." You say, "No, I can't. You do it. I already do so much for you." Your spouse says, "I don't think that's true at all. If our marriage really meant anything to you, you would do much more for me." This is a case of one person's judgment against another's. If you say "Yes" in this example and consequently don't stand by your own judgment, your relationship will be out of balance and the other person will be able to manipulate you to the absolute limit. A satisfactory solution is possible only if the judgments are weighed against each other and the two of you come to a compromise.

4. **Sovereignty of action.** You have the right to make mistakes. Your client says, "You've got to get the customer assessment finished over the weekend, no matter what it takes!" You say, "Impossible! My family is more important to me." Your client says, "That's no good. Your assessment last year had quite a few mistakes and now you've got to make up for it." Christ said, "Let him who is without sin cast the first stone." This is based on a fundamental truth: no one is perfect. If you have learned self-confidence, you can acknowledge an error, apologize, and work out a solution with other people. Don't let people keep on using your mistakes against you and make you work as a penalty.

5. **Sovereignty in making decisions.** You have the right to make illog-

ical decisions. Your spouse says, "You should stop working for the council." You say, "No, it's very important to me." Your spouse says, "I'm only thinking of you. You get very worked up and stressed." Your spouse argues in a logical and helpful way, but still manipulates you. Stick to your "No" and steer the conversation to your different needs. You are arguing from an emotional angle and your partner is being logical. Both are justified. On this basis you should find a compromise.

Seven Ways to Say "No" While Keeping Your Relationship with the Other Person

You can see the word "no" as the key word for more sovereignty, your own time management, and more satisfaction. In addition to the basic decision to be more self-aware, there are also a few proven simplification tips to make your "no" easier for the other person to deal with.

1. **"Give me some time to consider."** Or "Let me think about it. I'll call you back in an hour." Call back in an hour and say "No" politely and clearly without any further justification. The time you take to think about it and the fact that you honor your commitment to call back make your response seem less blunt.

2. **"That's a great offer!"** Show that you appreciate the request with a sentence of recognition. But then make it clear that your time is so taken up with something else at the moment that you must regretfully say "No" to this project. Don't explain what "something else" is or why it is more important. That could lead to a contradiction or even a dispute.

3. **"I value you so much!"** When you get a request or inquiry, commend the other person and strengthen your relationship. You then move into your rejection with the words: "There's no one I would rather do that with than you, but this time I have to say no."

4. **"That's something I don't do as a matter of policy."** People deal with a refusal more easily if they know that it is not meant person-

ally but rather as a matter of policy. "I never buy anything at the door." "I've hardly had any time for my family recently and I've had to set a clear priority there."

5. **"I'm really sorry for you!"** This refusal is especially helpful with indirect requests: "We would love to come with the whole family, but unfortunately the hotels are so expensive …." Don't read anything into the words. (He probably wants me to invite him to stay at my place.) Just respond to what the person has actually said and show understanding on the emotional level.

6. **"That doesn't suit me."** This is an empty sentence that just postpones the matter, but it satisfies some people. They drop their request. If they still insist, you can use another empty expression: "I'm afraid I can't say at the moment." The more personal the relationship, the more careful you should be with this option. If you are asked to do something on a particular day, instead of saying, "No, I don't feel like it," you can first try saying, "No, I can't do it that day." That won't be quite so unacceptable to the person.

7. **"Hmm … no."** This is the best method in the end. If you mean "No," then say "No"—with a clear pause beforehand that signals thought about it and consideration for the other person. Say "No" in a definite tone of voice and look at the person when you say it. Otherwise you make it look as though there is still room for negotiation. Don't add any justification or you encourage the other person to enter into a discussion. A clear reply saves you aggravation later. An advantage is that you avoid misunderstandings and the other person knows where you're coming from.

Simplifying Idea 13: Slow Down Your Life

Discover Creative Slowness

As we have already mentioned, each of us has 24 hours every day. But our personal clocks tick at different speeds. Some experts call the speed of your inner clock "own time" and they call your boss's, customer's, or family's time "others' time." A key step in the way of simplification is to bring these two rhythms into harmony with each other.

Find Your "Own Time"

Make a list showing which jobs you prefer and do best at which times of the day. Under what conditions do you work most effectively? What is your ideal time for going to bed and for getting up? Would you like to sleep after lunch?

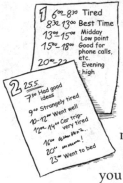

On a second list write down your working times for at least a week and assess the quality of your work subjectively. With these lists you will soon be able to discover which "time pattern" would be ideal for you. Work out with your boss, colleagues, and family how your working times could be optimized.

For example, you could shift meetings from the morning (your own individual peak time) to the early afternoon (your lowest point for working alone). Or you could agree with your employer and your family that you work three evenings at home (your most creative time) and in exchange you might have two afternoons just for your family.

Find Your Inner "Time Thief"

It's not only people around you who steal your time. Our own personality structure plays a much bigger role here than many people think. Here are the most important types of time-consuming structures:

Time thief 1: The high standard. Because of your personal values, you expect more from yourself than you can do in the time available.

The simplifying solution: Lower your standards. Switch your orientation away from others to self-determination. Your values that determine your standards are generally associated with your parents and upbringing. Imagine your parents in front of you and say, "Thank you for everything you have done for me. But now I am standing on my own two feet and I'm doing things my way."

Time thief 2: The 1,000 small jobs. You really want to get your tax return done—an important but unpleasant task. First you "just" go through the mail and you "just" make an appointment with the doctor and you "just" arrange to go to a concert that you're so looking forward to—and then half the day is gone.

The simplifying solution: Agree with yourself that you will spend one hour on the tax return and only then will you even think about something else. One hour is a manageable period that doesn't feel too oppressive. After an hour you will often find that you are so engrossed in the task that the 1,000 small jobs have lost their fascination.

Time thief 3: The super goal. Unrealistic expectations about possible goals can lead to chronic overstrain: "Next year, I'll be a millionaire" or "Once I've turned 45, I'll spend the rest of my life just playing golf." These are extreme examples, but they are becoming more common.

The simplifying solution: The best remedy for this type of overstrain is your spouse or partner. Talk about the future and what you expect from each other. It might turn out that your partner feels it's more important to have a decent life now than a luxurious life some time in the future.

Time thief 4: The nagging doubt. A vague feeling of dissatisfaction can induce you to overfill your day with appointments and tasks.

The first step is to pinpoint the sense of dissatisfaction. Look for a sense of it in your body. Which area occurs to you spontaneously? The

head? The heart? The stomach? The back? This gives a clue as to which issues you need to address in the second step.

If it's the *head*, the main issue will be self-doubt: existential fear, worries about the future, money problems.

The simplifying solution: You cannot solve your underlying problems of purpose with money or insurance policies. Start looking in a new direction and don't strive primarily for security; instead, look for happiness and satisfaction.

If it's the *heart*, the main issue will be social problems: lack of recognition, envying other people, lack of success, feeling that you're not needed.

The simplifying solution: Build and maintain real relationships with a few people. You will then find that the need for approval, praise, and success in business will recede by itself.

If it's the *stomach*, the main issue will be unexpressed annoyance or worry or anger: lack of strength, injustice, too much conflict, lack of quality of the environment (boss, company, work).

The simplifying solution: Express your annoyance out loud, bang the table, shout—but only for a short time. Then you can try to see the funny side of it. Rise above the issues and tell yourself, "Annoyances are a waste of time."

If it's the *back*, the main issue will be ongoing burdens: overstrain, extreme need for harmony, unresolved problems in your relationship and family.

The simplifying solution: Trust that you have an effect by your mere presence—not just through your actions. Try it! Go to meetings without having done your "homework." Leave things undone and admit quite openly how exhausted you are.

Time thief 5: The wrong way of working. You may have a sound *professional* training. But nobody has prepared you for the *way* to practice your profession. For people who work in a very individual way on teams, meetings and other situations where they have to consider others may seem a waste of time. When group-oriented people have to work at home, they often wait in vain for a brilliant idea and they waste a lot of time with uncreative frustration.

The simplifying solution: Find out whether you can do the same work better under very different conditions. Arrange with your boss a test phase in which you change from office work to field work, from working in the office to working at home, from a fixed contract to working on a freelance basis (or vice versa).

Time thief 6: The wrong job. If you continue in a job that doesn't suit you, just because you're afraid of unemployment, you will sooner or later become ill, mentally or physically. One of the main causes of time problems and overload is that people are doing the wrong jobs and they don't have the opportunity to use their abilities.

The simplifying solution: Think hard and ask yourself honestly which is the greater risk: losing your job or developing a psychosomatic illness, possibly for the rest of your life. Have the courage to make a change even if you're getting on in years. The job market is becoming more dynamic. There is a growing number of companies founded by people in their 50s and 60s who have left their former long-term jobs and who prefer to hire people from their own age group.

Combat Heart Disease

Over 500 working people were questioned in a representative survey by the opinion research institute EMNID for our monthly newsletter, *simplify your life®*. They were asked, "What aspect of your job gets on your nerves most?" One answer scored much higher than all the others: time pressure. Over 45% of those questioned said they were required to do more and more in less and less time. Among the readers of *simplify*, it was only 21%, but here too the problem of time pressure ranked as number one. This shows that time is the tightest resource in our society.

Many other studies (e.g., a major employee survey by INRA, a market and opinion research institute) confirm these results. Up to 80% of people would like less time pressure in their work. Here are three immediate measures to help you deal with time.

1. Work without a clock. Take your watch off. Do things now and then like children: get other people to remind you about appointments. Spend the time in between in a "time-free window." It is also very therapeutic to orient yourself exclusively to the chimes of a church clock. In the time between the quarter-hourly bells, live without any direct measurement of time. If there is no church clock near you, put an old-fashioned pendulum clock with a chime in the next room.

2. Relating to time as a garden. We use spatial images when we talk about time; usually these are expressions in which time is represented

in an active way while we are depicted as passive: "I'm under pressure" or "Time is pressing me" or "The deadline is looming over me." Change your inner images: imagine the time available to you as a garden that you are striding through. Here you can go as fast as you like, run around in a circle, try other ways, or just rest. The new image will allow your unconscious to change its perspectives: you are no longer ruled by time; you decide for yourself how to allocate your time.

3. Find your personal rhythm. Take time to do a little test. Sit on a chair and relax. Look at a clock and then close your eyes and do nothing for five minutes. During this time reflect on the fact that you are living *now*

and that the peaceful experience of these five minutes is something that nobody can ever take away from you again. When you think that five minutes have passed, open your eyes and look at the clock. Now you can see how fast you "tick."

If you had your eyes closed for less than four and a half minutes, your inner clock is running too fast. You tend to underestimate periods of time and pack your day too full. Allow yourself more slack time. Add a little to your calculations to give yourself more time.

If you had your eyes closed for more than five and a half minutes, you are ticking slower than the clock. You tend to create time reserves as a prudent measure and you "hoard" time. You run the risk of underestimating yourself and regarding time as an unalterable fate. Switch from "victim" to "doer." Trust yourself to take on more and you'll be amazed at the energy reserves you have within you.

Enjoy Time Now

Yesterday is history, tomorrow is a mystery, life is today! Don't spend time dreaming of the past and don't fantasize too much about the future. Simplify the way you experience time by concentrating on the present. Here are a few recommendations for extricating yourself from the type of worries and brooding that can make you ill.

Spend longer looking. While we're walking or traveling, we normally spend only a fraction of a second looking at everyday objects that we encounter. The day races past us without our really being aware of it. Scientists have discovered that the average time we spend looking at things has been steadily decreasing during the last 50 years. We tend to say that the world is going faster, but that might be because we are perceiving it faster.

Just try looking at objects for at least five seconds. Good opportunities for this exercise come when you're walking or looking out of the car or train window. You'll find that five seconds is a long time. Scientists have discovered that this slight increase in the time we take to observe things can appreciably increase our zest for life and the quality of life.

Say the names of things. Next time you go for a walk, do something that will strike you as a bit crazy: say out loud the names of things you see—blackbird, clouds, dandelion, gravel …. Children do that when they learn to speak. In this way, you activate both sides of the brain and you anchor the concepts in your memory. If you do this as an adult, it makes you more aware of the present and the feeling of being rushed decreases noticeably.

Slow routines down. Most people do unpleasant routine jobs quickly and carelessly to save time. But this just makes such tasks even more unpleasant, since the hasty manner of working doesn't yield any sat- isfaction. Try doing it differently: do repetitive jobs very slowly, enjoying them. Fill in a bank transfer slip very slow- ly and write "nicely." You will find that even boring rou- tines become a very conscious exercise. This makes your life richer and the lost time amounts to just a few seconds.

Breathe from your stomach. Consciously allow your stomach to extend when you breathe in. (You might have to loosen your belt.) Breathing with awareness is the basis of many forms of meditation and in stress- ful situations it brings you back from the "Something's being done to me" mindset to "Great, I'm alive!"

Eat with the other hand. Eat with your left hand if you are right-hand- ed or your right hand if you're left-handed. You'll eat more slowly and with more awareness and enjoyment because you'll have to pay more attention to make sure you don't drop anything.

Procrastination Is a Matter of Perspective

The bad habit of doing jobs at the last minute is so hard to get rid of because it's so hard to understand your nature. Neil Fiore, one of the great experts in the area of work organization, thought of a very dra- matic metaphor to illustrate the mechanism of procrastina- tion: the image of a plank. It's a matter of the perspec- tive from which you look at the plank.

Imagine it's your job to walk along a plank that is one foot wide and 30 feet long. The plank is lying on the ground. It wouldn't be too difficult, would it? You have all the skills to deal with the task. You would do it without a second thought.

First Variant: From Job to Catastrophe

Imagine the plank runs between two houses at a height of 100 feet above the street and you are asked to walk across.

Your adrenaline level will rise just contemplating it. One small mistake (even if it's very improbable that you would make a mistake) and the consequences would be disastrous. You find yourself paralyzed confronting your task.

In reality, it's you who's placed the plank at a height of 100 feet. You've raised the importance of a normal task to such a critical level that you're working under exceptional pressure and you feel that one error will be catastrophic.

Second Variant: From Madness to Heroism

Now imagine it differently. The plank is still situated at a dizzying height, but this time the house on your side is on fire. You can save your life only by getting across the plank as quickly as possible. Notice the difference: you would find creative solutions at once. You would sit down on the plank and slowly inch your way across it or take a run and make a dash for the other side without looking down.

Again, it's you who's set the house on fire. By postponing the task, you've put yourself under pressure. As a rule you'll manage the task—with stress, fear, and trepidation. But also with great satisfaction, because (as you discover) you've prevailed with great mastery over a magnificent challenge. If you had merely walked across the plank lying on the ground, you would never have had that sense of heroism.

That's the reason you will do it the same way next time (whether you consciously intend to or not). You remain in the vicious circle of procrastination. You will artificially increase the importance of the task and put yourself under pressure.

Third Variant: The Way out of the Vicious Circle

The plank is still situated at a dangerous height above the street, but the house is not on fire and there's a safety net under the plank that will definitely catch you if you fall. Now you can tackle the job and it will probably even be fun.

This safety net is your self-esteem. It's the best protection against your delaying tactic that sets the house on fire.

How to Cure Yourself of Procrastination

Avoid "I must" statements. Don't make them to yourself, either out loud or silently. When you say, "I must," your brain has to deal with two conflicting tasks: it has to make the energy available for the task and it has to protect you from the threat of possible failure. Your body prepares itself for fight and flight simultaneously—two energies that offset each other, leaving you disempowered.

A better solution is to say "I will" or "I can." And you must mean it. Say it out loud to yourself and others. Don't imagine yourself failing. Instead, imagine yourself having mastered the task successfully.

Concentrate on the beginning. If your mind knows that you are managing to do what you have taken on, you can let go of the goal while you are doing the task. That will seem strange to goal-oriented people. But concentrate on the beginning, the first step. Get absorbed in the doing instead of becoming obsessed with the end result. Develop a love of the journey—not just the destination.

Don't be perfect in your work. The wish for perfection is the reason people give most often for not trying something. Many people do not write a book because they know that it won't be perfect. People stick with their old, unhealthy, and badly paid job because they say, "The perfect job doesn't exist." It's better to align yourself with people who write (imperfect) books and have the courage to change to another (imperfect) job.

Play more. Some people punish themselves when they are under time pressure. They delete all the games on their PC, they stop going for walks, and they don't play with their kids in the evening. They then have less pleasure in life and less balance— and their work performance actually declines.

Break out of this pattern by paying more attention to relaxation and getting more involved in living when you are under pressure. Define clear time periods for this: half an hour for a walk, 10 minutes to play a game of solitaire on your PC. Your mind will become more creative during the recreational break and you will become more mentally fit. Free time without feelings of guilt will give you the strength to do high-quality work in the remaining time. Furthermore, a certain dose of recreation reduces the chances of developing stress-related disorders.

Interpret your fear correctly. At the beginning of a large project, you normally worry and feel anxious because in your thoughts you are already on the peak of the mountain and you see the tremendous height of the goal. Driven by this fear, many people just give up. It's helpful to learn that such fear is quite natural and that it should not cause you to give up, but rather it should motivate you to divide up the long path into manageable stages.

Work with a calendar in reverse. Write down the final deadline for your project on the first line of a piece of paper. Then, on each line, take one step back from the future toward the present. Of course, you could also enter the individual steps of the project in your normal calendar, going backward, but then you would be going against the psychological current. Your unconscious mind develops a natural aversion to doing that. The reverse calendar method works naturally: the project goes from the top (the final goal) downward (backward) and it takes on a structure that corresponds to its ultimate purpose. Use the reverse calendar method *often* if you feel overextended.

Work on worry. Worry slows us down and has a demotivating effect. Normally, when you are worrying, you just think of the possible problems ("It'll be disastrous if I deliver late again") and so you just stop at that point. It's usually enough to make you avoid the impending danger by running away. Working on worry means thinking further! Think up a worst-case scenario that could occur if you were to deliver too late. ("I would lose my job.") But don't just leave it there. Think further: what would I do if that happened? ("I would breath a sigh of relief" or "I would study and become a personal trainer.")

If you play all that out in a consistent way, you will have a big advantage over people who are afraid of failure: you will be aware that you have the resources to deal with that scenario. That gives you the self-confidence to negotiate the plank that spans the abyss in a spirit of fun instead of fear.

Delegate Consistently

On the list of time-saving activities, passing work to others comes right at the top. A lot of people say that delegating is only for managers. But people who regard themselves as solo workers can also benefit from delegating: the self-employed, one-person businesses, housewives, or employees at the bottom of a company hierarchy. There are at least five good reasons for delegating:

1. Delegating helps to promote and develop skills, initiative, and competence of coworkers.

2. Delegating in the family helps to support and develop independence in children.

3. Delegating means trusting others, thereby giving them confidence.

4. Delegating requires that you cooperate with others and it develops your social abilities.

5. Delegating helps you to simplify your life and to concentrate on the essential tasks.

You should know and observe the following basic rules that make delegating effective.

1. Transfer responsibility. Coworkers and children usually respond positively when they are given responsibility. That's why it's best not to dictate every step in tiny detail. For example, if you send a child shopping, give him or her a list that leaves room for decisions ("a nice piece of fruit," "your favorite sausage"). If you're not entirely satisfied with his or her choice, don't say anything. Give the child some room within which to exercise responsibility ("Don't spend more than $10").

2. Delegate challenges. Don't delegate with the thought "I must get rid of this unchallenging task." Instead, emphasize the appealing aspect of the job. In the shopping example, this might be "I'm interested to see whether you can take advantage of the special offers."

3. Delegate larger responsibilities with interim goals. It is particularly worthwhile to delegate medium- and long-term responsibilities. Allow sufficient time and check at regular intervals to make sure that the other person isn't overworked. For example, an archive for journals has to be organized and the time required for the job has been estimated at six days. On the second day, check whether your coworker has completed a third. If not, encourage him or her. It's not a good idea to wait until the sixth day and then ask whether everything is finished (while secretly anticipating failure).

Delegate on a daily basis as often and as much as possible. Don't delegate to just coworkers or family members, but also to other departments and external service providers (typing agencies, window cleaners, gardeners).

Delegate in Your Private Life as Well

The time you spend at home is valuable: being with your children or friends, physical fitness, meditation, self-improvement, and many other activities are priceless. Instead, you spend vast amounts of time doing shopping, housework, cleaning, and repairs. Learn from business professionals and adopt their habits in your private life.

Employ a driver. At first, this might sound snobbish. But work out very  carefully how much time you could save if someone were to do your shopping for you. And then there are the many odd jobs: getting books from the library and returning them, taking letters and packages to the post office, dropping film off to be developed and picking it up, taking laundry to the cleaners ....

If you do the shopping yourself, you might not make many stops, because you want to save time by buying all the items at once, in an expensive shop nearby. You can send a paid driver to supermarkets farther away. The price savings can cover part of the fee you pay the driver.

A lot of young people like to drive. You probably make a shopping list anyway as a simplifying measure, so why not shop the old-fashioned way, by hiring an "errand boy"? You may be able to find an ad posted in a local store. Talk to the young person's parents before you make any arrangements.

For insurance reasons, it's best if your driver uses his or her own car. The best option is to offer your driver-shopper a set price for all purchases. Alternatively, you could contact a professional; look in the yellow pages under "courier and delivery services."

Have things delivered. There is an increasing number of bookstores, both conventional and online, that deliver books directly to your house; you can place orders by phone or fax or often by e-mail or online.

If you have your newspaper delivered, why not have the bread delivered as well? Ask around or look in the yellow pages to find out whether there is a breakfast delivery service in your area. You don't have to make a special trip to the bakery for croissants, etc.

There are now mail-order companies for nearly everything: office supplies, clothing, wine, furniture. It is especially worthwhile having things delivered that you don't enjoy searching for in shops and that you can easily order from a catalog. If nobody is at home during the day and you don't have any neighbor who can take delivery, have your purchases delivered to your workplace.

Stop the Disruptions

This is a problem that can occur equally at home or at work: you've started something, you're in the midst of your work, and you get interrupted. It might be a colleague, a superior, a subordinate, someone calling on the phone, a visitor, your spouse, or the children.

You can avoid the typical interruptions if you use the right techniques. It's possible to apply a remedy without making yourself unpopular with other people.

Simplified Ways of Preventing Interruptions for Managers

Close your door. The permanently "open door" as a sign of positive relationships is now out of fashion with management pros. The thinking is now more flexible in top management. The door is closed when important things have to be dealt with or planning work is in progress or decisions are being made. The door is open when interruptions won't cause a problem. In American companies, managers leave the door ajar to keep potential disturbances at a distance while giving staff the signal that they can speak to the manager about really important matters.

"Out times." Arrange with your staff that you don't want to be disturbed during certain times of the day. This should also apply to visitors from outside. Get your secretary or switchboard to shield you. No appointments are made for this time and no calls are put through. If you work alone, put the answering machine on during these times.

"In times." You should also specify a particular time of day when your staff can speak with you. Keep to these times so that the new habit becomes established with the staff.

Problem box. To avoid disturbing you, anyone with questions should write them out in the form of a short note and put them in a box by your door. After your "out time," deal with this box first.

Let's be honest ... A manager who complains about not getting down  to anything should work in a cabin in the mountains or a health resort and develop a vision of the future for the company! A good manager can leave the business alone for two weeks. All work areas should be organized in such a way that staff members solve problems on their own.

Simplified Ways of Preventing Interruptions for Staff Who Are Disturbed by the Manager

A lot of managers still expect their staff to drop everything when they call for them. And yet staff often then have to wait until the manager finishes a telephone call or says goodbye to a visitor. The following measures can be useful.

Take work with you. Where possible, take documents with you that you can work on while you're waiting for the manager. In this way you can make the best use of the time as well as making a positive impression.

Advance planning. Be proactive instead of reactive. With important projects, don't wait until the manager calls you. Take the initiative and suggest meeting at a time convenient for both of you. The advantage is that you have time to prepare and this saves time for both parties.

Let's be honest ... Think carefully. Is your manager really the one who disturbs your work? If he or she is well organized, sets clear objectives,  defines priorities, and disturbs you only for good reasons, then he or she is not taking your time. If you nevertheless consider it a disturbance when he or she arrives on the scene, there's probably another reason. You might be linking some very different type of frustration with your boss. Try to discover the real reasons. You might need to change your job or gain self-confidence.

Simplified Ways of Preventing Interruptions for Colleagues and Peers

Be diplomatic. Try to come to a mutual understanding and regular communication at arranged times. Explain to your colleagues that, because of your body clock, you work best during a particular time of day. Hang a notice on the door: "Please do not disturb between 2:00 and 4:00." Agree with colleagues on a set time each day or week when matters of common concern relating to work can be discussed.

Set a good example. Whatever you do, don't distract other colleagues from their work by just appearing in the door-  way unannounced. Call them and arrange a time. In this way you can slow down (in a helpful way) an "everything immediately" culture.

Be clear and unambiguous. If a chatterbox is standing in your doorway, just turn your head toward him or her and say in a friendly but quite definite way, "I'm at a tricky point right now and I need to get this done for a client today. Then I'll have a little breathing room. Thanks for understanding." You give a nice smile, nod, and then get back to your work *immediately*.

Avoiding small talk. Maintain the social network in the morning, at lunchtime, and at the end of the day with small  talk for clearly limited periods of time; in this way you show that you're willing to mix with colleagues as well as that you respect them. Some interruptions by colleagues are instinctive attempts to make sure of the solidarity of the group. Five minutes each day are quite sufficient for this purpose.

Let's be honest .... Think carefully. How big is your own part in the interruptions? Do you love a little chat? Are you afraid that it will offend others if you set boundaries or that you will become an outsider? Could it be that your work is either too much or not challenging enough and so you are subconsciously open to interruptions?

Simplified Ways of Preventing Interruptions for All Office Workers Who Interrupt Themselves

The more boring, complicated, and tedious a task, the greater the temptation to avoid the unpleasant work with interruptions that you engineer yourself. But sooner or later you have to deal with the matter and then you have to pay the price for the interruptions: you work under pressure, you feel unhappy, and you might not deliver the best quality. Here are the most common types of self-interruption in offices and what you can do about them.

Separate the private sphere. Problem: You like to visit colleagues for a private chat. ("Ms. Smith is having problems with her son.")

The simplifying solution: Meet outside office hours, e.g., during the lunch break.

Stay in one place. Problem: You visit another department or branch even though it isn't necessary or the matter could be sorted on the phone.

The simplifying solution: Try for two weeks to consistently use the phone to solve problems. Regard every phone call as "saved travel time."

Restrict creative breaks. Problem: You wander around the office or other places on your floor in order to reflect. ("I just get more ideas when I'm talking to other people.")

The simplifying solution: Go over to the window and spend three minutes looking out. At the same time, give the edge of your ear a vigorous massage, from top to bottom, three times. That massage (the so-called "thinking cap") refreshes and activates the brain.

Avoid hold-ups. Problem: You frequently go to the photocopier or other shared equipment when they're in greatest demand. ("I had to wait in line so long.")

The simplifying solution: Find out when the photocopier is free and do several copying operations at once. Better still, delegate the task.

Restrict meetings. Problem: Discussions and meetings with colleagues and staff drag on and on. ("We must get to know each other better and keep in touch.")

The simplifying solution: Invite only those members of staff who really have something to do with the project. Define the subjects clearly beforehand and set a time limit. If you are not the organizer of the meeting, you can set this limit individually: "I need to be away by 3:00 p.m."

Simplified Ways of Preventing Interruptions for All Home Workers Who Interrupt Themselves

If you work alone, you are free from a lot of disturbances that typically occur at the office. On the other hand, you have to keep motivating yourself. Here are the most frequent problems.

Keep a notepad for ideas. Problem: When something goes on for a long time, you suddenly get a lot of good ideas for other projects. ("I'm just a creative scatterbrain. You've got to listen to your inspiration.")

The simplifying solution: Keep an "ideas notepad for brainstorms" or a dictating machine ready. Put down a brief outline of the idea and the date. Then return to your current task immediately.

Offering rewards. Problem: You get into computer games or surf the Internet longer than necessary.

The simplifying solution: Be consistent in using computer games and Web-surfing as self-reward. ("When I have done this and that, I'll allow myself one game of Monkey Island on the computer.") There is an old, ridiculously simple remedy to keep Internet searching from getting out of hand: set an alarm clock to bring you back to reality in 20 minutes!

The best trick when you get "writer's block." Problem: You have to write something and you find the beginning so difficult that you sit there paralyzed in front of the screen or the blank sheet of paper in front of you.

The simplifying solution: Don't start with the first sentence; start with the second or third. If you're using a PC, it's no problem to insert the

first sentence later—and generally it will flow effortlessly from the keyboard when you have finished the rest of the text. If you're writing on paper, just leave some space above the first lines that you write.

Get a running start. Problem: You are faced with a task that you don't like doing.

The simplifying solution: Use a template as the equivalent of getting a running start before jumping over something. Open a similar file that you can overwrite or find a hard copy document that could serve as a model or template that you can easily copy and just change individual words. You'll see that, after a short while, you'll be able to get a start from the model text, rather like a ski jumper takes off from the ramp, and you'll be able to formulate your own text.

Brainstorming. Start off with brainstorming in writing. Force yourself to spend five minutes writing down on a blank sheet of paper individual concepts around your subject. Then you use lines to connect the things that belong together and draw a line around the idea you want to begin with.

Simplified Ways of Dealing with Interruptions by Visitors and Customers

Get to the point. Restrict the initial greeting to a few friendly words. Whatever you do, don't steer the conversation to general issues or personal matters. Don't ask, "How have you been lately?" Start in a matter-of-fact way: "What did you need to see me about?"

Use body language. Don't offer uninvited guests anything to drink. Don't make yourself comfortable. Don't settle down and lean back in your chair; sit upright.

The trick with the watch. At the beginning of the visit, set a clear time frame, according to the importance of your guest. ("We've got 10 minutes/just under an hour, so let's get straight to the point!") Make sure the other person can see a clock in your room from where he or she is sitting. Here's a particularly effective tip: after setting the time frame, take off your watch and place it front of you, openly and obviously.

Close with a compliment. Give your guest the feeling that you appreciate him or her and that, for you, esteem has nothing to do with time. At the end of the meeting, come up with some praise. That makes the parting less difficult.

Deal with things immediately. If a problem can be solved immediately, do it. If not, delegate it to a member of staff or ask the guest for a written summary of the most important points.

Preventive measures. Arrange with your secretary or colleagues to contact you about an "urgent" matter after 15 minutes at the latest if you receive an unannounced visitor.

Indicate the end. Give clear signals when you want the meeting to end: close your time planner, start shuffling papers on your desk, move forward in your chair. Summarize the result of the meeting in one sentence and then say, "I think we have taken a step forward. I have enjoyed your visit." Your guest will recognize the signals and get up. Stand up at the same time.

The emergency brake. If necessary, end the meeting very clearly by adopting a positive facial expression, clapping your hands, and saying, "I think we've now resolved everything." Then stand up briskly.

See your guest out. A guest will judge you less by the number of minutes you have allowed him or her than by the last impression you give. Accompany your guest to the door, to the elevator, or to his or her car. That will convey the feeling that you are doing something for him or her. In this way you can turn a 10-minute meeting into a very positive experience for your guest.

Plan ahead. If the meeting takes longer than planned, ask your visitor to make an appointment for another meeting, so that you have more time for him or her.

Get Over Your Reluctance to See Things Through

One of the typical phenomena with people who have a tendency to disorder in their lives is the refusal to complete a task they have started. The classic example is not replacing the cap on the toothpaste tube after using it. Other manifestations of the reluctance to see things through include the following:

- Leaving the remains of food and packaging in the car after eating.
- Putting change into jacket pockets instead of a purse.
- Not hanging up coats and other clothing after taking them off.
- Not putting dirty wash in the laundry basket immediately.
- Not putting tools away after using them.

Just think—these behaviors never save time. The objects have to be cleared away sooner or later. But in the meantime, there is chaos that makes life unnecessarily difficult.

The 30-Second Principle

A lot of people who have a tendency to disorder feel agitated. Faced with a lot of tasks that await them, they say, "Not now!" to the job in

front of them and they overestimate the time it would take. Use a kitchen clock timer or a stopwatch to find out how long it takes to do the tasks you avoid because you don't like them. If you discover that it only takes 20 seconds to hang a jacket up, you will be more inclined to do it in the future. It takes four minutes to vacuum a room and it takes about three minutes to iron a shirt.

Apply the 30-second principle to get over the reluctance to see things through. If it takes 30 seconds or less to do a job, do it at once. If you keep to this rule, your car and your house will soon look much tidier—and they will stay that way.

Stem the Flood of Information

We are spending more and more time with media. There is no ebb in the flow of information and entertainment. Every new medium appears with a promise to simplify our lives, but none of the old media really fade away. Find your way of simplification here; pick among the following suggestions the ones that suit you best.

Reduce Your "Must Read" Pile

Don't encumber yourself with stacks of unread newspapers, magazines, brochures, and catalogues. If there's more in the pile than you could read in one month, it will just be a psychological burden. Go through all the papers, keep the three most interesting, and dispose of the rest. You can bet your bottom dollar that you will feel a sense of relief. It's best to read the three saved papers the same day and then throw away as much as possible. (See the next tip.)

Read Magazines with a Knife

When you find an informative article in a magazine, cut it out. That way you avoid adding the magazine to the pile "because there's something in it I want to read."

Put Your Own Index in Books

When you find something interesting in a book, make your own index (with page numbers) on the inside of the back cover. That will make it easy to find the "good bits" again. It will also help you to read in a more conscious and structured way.

If that seems too laborious, colored labels will do the job (e.g., 3M index tabs). As a rule you will find three to 10 places in a book that you will want to refer to again later. The colored labels (which should ideally stick out at the top) will enable you to find those places quickly. You can also see at a glance that you have read this book intensively.

This applies to novels as well as non-fiction books. If there's something that you find very moving in a novel, put a sticker on it!

Don't Read Daily Newspapers

Reading the newspaper at breakfast is a cherished habit. The information content is usually minimal. Even good daily papers usually have only one article that stimulates you so much that you will tell other people about it during the course of the day. And let's be honest: what would be lost if you didn't read that article?

A trick for simplification: delegate the newspaper reading to another member of the family. If there's something really interesting, he or she will soon let you know about it. You can get the daily information from the car radio, the kitchen radio (a good place for listening to the radio), or the evening news. At breakfast, it's better to read journals, preferably selected articles. Or, even better, use this time for communication with your family. Work meetings are essential in professional life; in private life, the equivalent is the "breakfast conference."

If you can't let go of your newspaper, just read selected parts that contain useful information (e.g., the business section or political commentary). Don't even browse through the rest. The time it takes is enormous compared with the result.

Notebook Instead of Lots of Bits of Paper

When you make a note of something, write it either in your time planner or in a small notebook for things that you must not forget. Lots of little pieces of paper scattered around will tend to distract your concentration. Whoever scatters notes becomes scattered by the notes!

Reduce Ordinary Advertising Materials

T-shirts and caps with advertising printed on them, coffee cups with brand slogans, amusing sayings on the fridge, pens with corporate information, and a thousand other objects around you are constantly sending messages that disturb your unconscious. Ban these diversions from your field of vision. For example, you can transfer cornflakes from the loud packaging to a simple large glass container.

Put Children's Books on Display

To motivate children and young people to read, do what booksellers do: put one or two books on the shelf with the front cover facing forward, alternating the titles on a weekly basis. That sends a message to the child, "Cool! I've got that one, too!" and it sends a subliminal message that "Books are important."

Read the Information Services

Here's a bit of advertising for us for a change. We went through about 650 German and American books in preparation for this book—a set of shelves six and a half feet high and six and a half feet wide full of books. In the several hundred pages of this book, you get a summary of a whole stack of books a good 40 feet high, which would cost over $8,500 and a lot of time reading.

In addition, there are services that can be enormously helpful in optimizing the information you acquire. Top managers have been using them for a long time. The online service *www.getAbstract.com* (paid subscription) is outstanding for business.

Cure Your Television Addiction

There is nothing wrong with watching television. There is no other medium that communicates to all the senses so intensively and memorably. A study carried out in Sweden in 1995 actually showed that children from households without a television were disadvantaged in matters of general education and practical intelligence in comparison with "television children," provided the latter didn't just sit continuously in front of the box. Sitting glued to the television destroys the positive effects of television. Here are a few simplifying tips for using the TV in a helpful way.

Watch a program and then take a break. Never just turn on the television. First, find a particular program that you want to watch. Make a decision that you are going to turn it off *immediately* after this program and that you will withstand all requests to "Stay tuned!" This is particularly important when you are alone in a hotel room and tempted to turn on the television to counteract the unfamiliar experience of solitude.

The trick of just going away. Sometimes you get caught up in a film that is really worthless and sit in front of the box although you are not even enjoying it. The remedy: leave the room while the television is still on. Once the "magic thread" is broken, it will be easier to realize that the film isn't worth watching. Go back into the room and turn the television off.

Delegating television. When you want to watch a particular program
 because it may be of interest to you in connection with work or hobbies, ask someone else to watch the program and record it on video. Later you can ask the person which bits (if any) would be interesting for you. You need only watch those bits on video.

The 50% withdrawal. Break the series addiction. Daily soaps and other television series can be addictive. If you've become addicted, just watch every other episode. That way you still get the plot, but you save time and it will be easier to get away from it after a while.

Away with rituals! Rethink your television rituals. Can't you live with-
 out the TV news? Develop alternatives like listening to the news from a public radio station; they usually give more detailed bulletins than television stations. That way you can keep TV news from becoming like a "gateway drug" that leads you into the evening programs.

Simplify Your Communication

Not many people like to write. When people have to do some writing, they tend to put it off for a long time. The most important advice for simplification in this area is to aim low! Don't write perfectly; go for half-perfect and don't worry about questions of style or spelling mistakes. Get the unpleasant task done, the sooner the better. Here are a few proven simplification tips.

Make Written Memos Easier

"Write me a report about it." This has been an epidemic in the United States for a long time. Try to convince your manager that the information content is the important thing, not the appearance. In many cases, a copy of the important document (letter, prospectus, newspaper article) with a few handwritten comments is the simplest solution.

Write in a Simpler and More Colorful Way

Business letters are often like a museum for habits of bygone times, such as "You are respectfully requested," "Please find enclosed," and "Yours faithfully." Even personal letters contain phrases that have long become obsolete and even friendly greetings are sometimes expressed in a stiff and monotonous way.

Take the mustiness out of your letters! It's hard at first, but after a short while you will see that the new style of writing is more pleasant, that unpleasant correspondence is easier, and that the recipients are happier to read your letters.

Use all your senses. Write what you see, hear, taste, and feel. Also, stick to this ideal for writing letters: write as you speak.

Simplify Your E-Mail

"You have 35 new messages." More and more people are greeted by their computer at work with such notifications. In some companies staff are trained by specialists just so that they can deal with e-mails and then get on to their other activities. One of these specialists is  Nathan Zeldes, productivity manager at Intel Israel. Here is his advice.

Delete without opening. Check through the sender and the subject of any incoming messages listed before you read the individual messages. You can delete many messages unread. Some e-mail programs have filters that enable you to reject at the outset certain types of undesirable messages. E-mails with subject lines in capital letters, for example, are virtually always advertising.

Put things into baskets. Reproduce a sensible paper system on your PC. Don't misuse the inbox for miscellaneous storage; after reading messages, sort them into project-related mailboxes.

Reply immediately. Take advantage of the greatest benefit of e-mail: the

quick reply. This should become second nature to you. After you read a message, either reply or delete it. If you have to do some work before giving a full reply, write an intermediate message.

Set up a five-week mailbox. On your PC you should set up something akin to the "pre-wastebasket" in a paper-based office. The "five-week" mailbox is for messages when you are unsure whether the sender will get back to you or messages that you could use for other purposes. Go through this file every five weeks and delete anything that you've dealt with.

Invent abbreviations. Agree with colleagues on abbreviations to use in

the subject line so the recipient can quickly see what the message is about. Here are some examples. "To do" or "AR" (action required) for important matters that have to be dealt with. "Info" or "FIO" (for information only) for things that are not so urgent.

Use "e-mail short messages." Messages that can be given just in the subject line are very practical. After the subject line, write "EOM" (end of message) or "NFM" (no further message) so that the recipient doesn't have to open your e-mail. Such short messages are particularly suitable for confirming receipt: "Many thanks for your prompt reply (NFM)."

Notify others when you'll be away. Finding hundreds of unopened e-mails on your return from vacation is not an inevitable fate. Most e-mail programs include the out-of-office feature. Anyone who sends you an e-mail receives a response indicating why he or she will not receive an immediate reply and when you will be back.

Use "carbon copy" sparingly. E-mails can be sent easily to a large group of recipients. That's what many people like to do, in order to cover themselves on all sides. Establish a policy in your company that "cc:" should be used only in exceptional cases, since excessive use of "carbon copy" is primarily to blame for e-mail glut.

Attention to attachments. Another bad habit: attaching image and other huge files. Do this sparingly and only if you know that the recipient needs this file in this size. Otherwise, it's more polite to excerpt the corresponding passages and send only those. If you send images, they should be only those that serve as information and you should first reduce the screen format (to a maximum of 700 pixels high) and save color images in the space-saving JPG format.

If you use a Web-based e-mail program, as soon as you see large messages in your list of incoming e-mails, first open the e-mails and check what kind of attachment is involved before you take all the time to download it to your PC.

Express yourself concisely. You should make it a goal to write e-mails as short and concise as possible. When you reply, quote the other person's message only if it is absolutely necessary and then only relevant excerpts. That makes it simpler for the other person to read your e-mail—and, after all, e-mail was invented for the purpose of simplification.

Simplifying Idea 14: Escape Now and Then

When you are faced with a task that you can come to grips with only on your own, there's just one thing to do: escape! Successful, creative people all have their refuges where they withdraw in order to work. But it doesn't have to be Ernest Hemingway's bungalow overlooking the sea. Here are a few suggestions for this simplification trick, a second office.

In the back seat of a car. When the weather allows (not too hot, not too cold), set up your office in the car. Drive to a remote spot where you won't be disturbed and sit in the back. (That's the trick.) Now you are no longer the driver—you're the boss!

In the open air. Depending on the weather, you might set up your second office in a park, by a lake, or in another inspiring natural spot.  Some people have an instinctive disinclination: "Working in a place like that? That's where I want to relax!" But they underestimate the enormous energy that comes from such a positive place. Don't worry: you won't ruin the lovely place with your work. It's actually the other way around: the lovely environment will make your work more pleasant and enjoyable.

Deserted places. Almost every company has unused premises: large meeting rooms, a canteen (between mealtimes), empty offices, or at least the desk of an field sales representative that is open from time to time. (You could ask in advance when you can use his or her desk.) It's important that the place be as far as possible from your office. Then tell people about your absence as if you were going out and switch the answering machine on or do whatever you normally do when you are going to be out. You will have two or three hours without interruption in which you can do wonders.

"Power places." There is a Microsoft advertisement in which a woman disappears into a church with a Notebook PC so that she can at last work undisturbed. If you were not the only person in the church, the sound of the keyboard would certainly be a problem. However, the basic idea is very intelligent: finding powerful places that have a positive effect on your concentration and inspiration. If you can get by with a book and pad of paper, you won't disturb anyone. Good alternatives to the ecclesiastical environment include a public library, an old-fashioned café (where you can sit in peace), a self-service restaurant (with no waiters to disturb you), a museum, or a hotel foyer.

The train. Find out which places enhance your creativity. For me it's the train. When I know that I'm going to be traveling for four hours with-

out phone calls and people knocking on my door, I find my mind is free
and I can read or write complex articles. If necessary,
it can even be the line that goes to the airport, which
I can use as often as I like with a monthly pass. There
can be problems working on the train, of course: if the
train is overcrowded (always on Friday and Saturday
afternoons), if the person sitting opposite you keeps talking
away, if there's a loud group of tourists in the compartment, or if train
trips make you tired (some people fall asleep after a few miles).

In the air. Other people work best in airplanes. However, the disruptive
procedures (checking in, waiting, boarding, taking off, landing, disem-
barking, waiting for luggage) are tough on any inner concentration.
Also, this method doesn't work as well for shorter flights.

The Place of Your Dreams

Look for other unused places in which you're protected you from disturbances, places that allow you to focus completely on a *single* priority. You'll see: even the search for such a place is a creative act that is
rewarding.

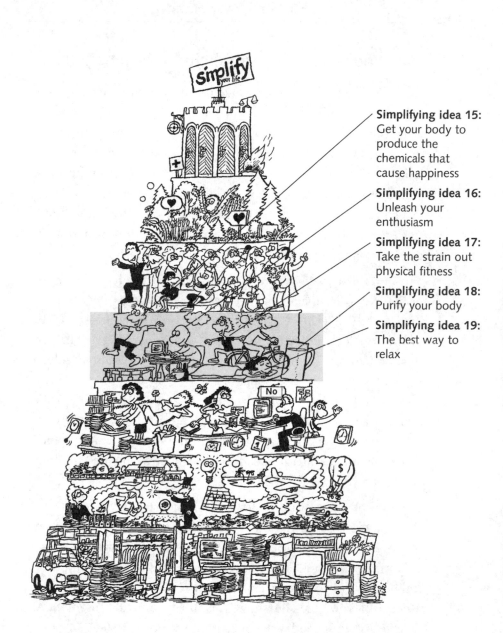

Simplifying idea 15:
Get your body to produce the chemicals that cause happiness

Simplifying idea 16:
Unleash your enthusiasm

Simplifying idea 17:
Take the strain out physical fitness

Simplifying idea 18:
Purify your body

Simplifying idea 19:
The best way to relax

Step 4 of Your Life Pyramid:
Simplify Your Health

Your Dream of Simplicity: Fifth Night

Now free from many minor and major burdens in your life, you float up to the fourth level of your pyramid as though you were weightless. Underneath you is the porous wall with your activities, constantly surrounded by the clock faces, which now seem much further away. You notice how you have been coming closer and closer to yourself. Among all the things and money, you had hardly noticed yourself. On the third level, which was about time, you saw that the wall that is gradually being worn away is directly connected with you.

On the fourth level, you find that you are pervaded by a sense of home and intimacy that you have never known before. At a first glance, it seems as though this part of the edifice consists only of mirrors. Wherever you look, you see only yourself: one moment from a distance and then close up. You see individual parts of your body and sometimes you can even see through your skin. Familiar smells are wafting around you. As you walk around, you feel a pleasant warmth and also an icy coldness, sometimes a pleasant tingling sensation and then a sharp pain. One moment you are tired and weary; the next you are bubbling with energy.

In some places you see poles, pipes, and strange connections that apparently lead to other levels of the pyramid. You are on the level of your physical health and, of course, all your illnesses. You already knew it: there are connections among your physical health and your finances, your possessions, and many other aspects of your life. But now you are astonished about how diverse these dependencies are, how the fourth stage of your pyramid is constantly being moved back and forth, up and down by a tangle of restless links.

While you are looking at all this, you make a surprising discovery: as soon as you examine one of the connections more carefully and consider where it could lead, it becomes thinner and weaker; some shrink away completely. You hear your body breathe a sigh of relief; a small current of happiness flows through you. And again you sense what you are going to do at this level of your life pyramid.

Simplifying Objective for Step 4

Learn to listen to your body and conserve your energies.

"If you've got your health, you've got everything!" say many people. And they usually mean the absence of illness. However, health is more than that—and also, at the same time, less.

Being healthy means more than just not being ill. People are healthy when they have a sense of well-being in their body and derive happiness from physical exertion, when they look after and cultivate their physical energies.

But being healthy also means being allowed to be ill. Your illnesses are inextricably linked to your psychological growth. In the same way that childhood illnesses play a decisive part in development, one of the important abilities for an adult is to understand and make use of signals from the body. People who use drugs or other medical remedies to eliminate symptoms the moment they appear are depriving themselves of a valuable resource for inner maturation and a deeper understanding of others. Furthermore, it can be dangerous to refuse to look for the actual cause of an illness and not to get to the root of the problem.

There is hardly any other level of your life pyramid where making a positive start is as important as it is here. That is why we show you a few simplification steps with which you can achieve happiness and contentment in a very simple way.

Simplifying Idea 15: Get Your Body to Produce the Chemicals That Cause Happiness

Get Some Physical Exercise

Make sure you get at least half an hour of normal physical exercise every day, preferably in the fresh air. Good ways of doing this include

cycling, going for walks, gardening, jogging, or any other type of physical activity that you enjoy, as well as just normal walking.

Physical exercise causes beta-endorphins to be released in the body. These endogenous peptides regulate the transmission of information between nerve cells and brain cells and have an effect that is distantly related to opium: they dispel depressive moods and decrease your awareness of pain. The ideal activity, by the way, would be dancing, which combines the positive effect of music with social contact.

Whenever you see an escalator or an elevator, automatically say to yourself, "Not me!" and look for the stairs. Using the stairs is the cheapest and most effective fitness exercise. When you reach the top or the bottom, you will feel your heart pounding, but you will also have a healthy sense of satisfaction.

Sense the Sky

Look up at the sky at least once every day, totally aware. Get a sense of the expansiveness of the sky and the universe around you; at the same

time, breathe deeply and easily and feel the ground beneath your feet. In this way you really can free yourself from the burdens and pressures of the tasks that are weighing upon you. Incidentally, when you stand facing east, you are pointing in the direction the earth is traveling in. The earth is turning that way and you are turning with it—and, depending on your latitude in the United States, you're moving at over 700 miles per hour!

Experts on the subject of happiness advise us to get up early at least once every month and go out into the country to watch the sunrise. Further endorphin-producing activities include walking barefoot on wet grass, swimming in the open air (in a lake or a heated open-air swimming pool), or enjoying the still-  ness in nature. If you have a particularly hard day ahead of you, get up earlier than usual and wander through open fields for half an hour.

If you find the difficulties of a task too much and it is affecting your motivation, say to yourself, "Stop!" Shift your body around a little and look up at the sky. Go out into the open air or at least go to a window. Look upwards until the focus of your vision is infinity.

Think back at the same time. When have I managed a similar task successfully? Who and what helped me at that time? Be aware of your own part in the success and don't attribute everything to luck and chance. Even the smallest positive recollection of your own abilities can serve as an impetus to motivate you and to lift you out of a negative mood that impairs your abilities.

Keep Well by Smiling

Start each day with a smile in front of the mirror. That sounds silly at first, but it has been well researched and the positive effect has been proven. A good, genuine smile (where the eye and cheek muscles are tensed for about 30 seconds) gives the brain a signal: watch out—there's a reason to be in a good mood! The basic principle underlying this facial feedback practice is that simulating a feeling can actually pro-duce the feeling.

This also helps with the experience of frustration or events that spoil your positive mood. People benefit when they smile. It's the best weapon against mobbing (collective psychological and emotional abuse)!

It's also good to smile when you go to sleep. It's dark, no one sees it—but you feel it.

Become Happy by Sleeping

A good, deep sleep increases our ability to be happy. A few simple rules will help: no heavy food for dinner, don't eat anything after 8:00 p.m., if necessary drink a cup of a soothing tea or a glass of warm milk before going to bed, have a regular ritual for going to sleep, make sure the room is well ventilated, possibly a comfortable blanket, don't have 110/120V electrical devices by the bed (use a battery-operated clock instead of a radio alarm clock!). The tip to replenish your energy in a simple and effective way: go to bed before 10:00 p.m. at least once a week.

If you have problems going to sleep, try one of the recognized relaxation meditations. We have selected two particularly good ones.

Eagle meditation. Imagine yourself high up on a rock from which you  can look out far across the evening landscape. In front of you, you can see an eagle in its nest. It slowly spreads its wings and takes off with great power. Calmly moving its wings, it soars and glides toward the evening sun. You follow every movement of its wings. You watch very intensively and carefully until it is no more than a tiny point on the horizon.

Escalator meditation. You are standing on a moving sidewalk, the type of horizontal escalator used in airports. But the sidewalk you are standing on has no end. It carries you calmly, at a constant speed, out of the airport until you find yourself in the open air. You go past beautiful landscapes, over past a river, through a forest. The sidewalk takes you farther and farther, until you come to a wide beach. You are carried farther and farther, along the shore, down the endless, secluded, beautiful beach while the fiery red sun slowly sinks into the ocean.

Eat Yourself Happy

Despite all the warnings, the truth is that nothing con-
tributes to our well-being as much as eating, from
earliest childhood in fact.

Well-being, however, is never a result of
quantity, but only of quality. Be choosy about
what you allow into your body. It has now
been scientifically proven many times: food nourishes not only the
body but also the mind. Our simplification list tells you what food has
which positive side effect.

Simplifying Nutritional Tips for Body and Mind

- **Improves concentration:** avocados, asparagus, carrots, grapefruit
- **Strengthens muscles and the brain:** herring, ocean perch
- **Enhances memory:** milk, nuts, rice
- **Improves your mood:** orange juice, paprika, soybeans, bananas
- **Reduces stress:** cottage cheese, almonds, brewer's yeast
- **Enhances well-being:** beans, peas, tofu
- **Helps sleep:** bread, noodles
- **Good for social skills:** lobster, wheat germ

- **Strengthens the immune system:** garlic
- **Increases sexual desire:** oysters, morels, pulse (peas, beans, lentils)
- **Protects against heart disease and cancer and improves your mood:** a glass of red wine in the evening

Simplifying Idea 16: Unleash Your Enthusiasm

The great discovery of the Hungarian-American psychologist Mihaly
Csikszentmihalyi, the leading expert in research on happiness and creativity, is that happiness or unhappiness depends not so much on the
circumstances of your life but on you.

You cannot manufacture happiness. But neither is happiness something that simply happens, inevitably, like fate. The simple truth lies between these two ideas: happiness is a state for which you can prepare yourself. You cannot cause happiness, true, but you can effectively prevent it. Csikszentmihalyi summarizes the situation: "People who learn to control inner experiences will be able to determine the quality of their lives, which is as close as any of us can come to being happy."

People don't experience the greatest happiness on a deckchair on the beach when they are on vacation. The best moments in life are not the passive or relaxed times; they occur when mind and body are exerted to the limits. You experience happiness when you discover a flame of curiosity and kindle it until it becomes a fire of enthusiasm. Happiness is never a permanent condition; it is made up of individual conditions that give rise to happiness. Csikszentmihalyi calls this condition "flow": becoming so absorbed in an activity that nothing else seems to matter—like children during an intense game. When you are in the flow, things happen by themselves, they go smoothly and effortlessly. Flow is associated with inner simplicity; you could say that it is the experience of simplicity itself. When you are in the flow, there is order in your consciousness.

Every phase of our life involves typical experiences of happiness that cannot be repeated, like being in love for the first time. It would be ridiculous for married people to keep expecting to repeat the thrill of the first meeting. Don't be too ready to believe people who claim that they are "in love just like they were on the first day." Real happiness does not arise out of a longing for the past; it comes from further development of the mind—for example, the happiness of having children, of having achieved something with a lasting effect, or of being able to enjoy life despite a physical limitation.

The experience of happiness is completely independent of culture, age, education, or prosperity. Csikszentmihalyi found people who were happier than average among miners, artists, managers, and surgeons. Almost all of them were hard-working and thought about their lives.

Seven Simplification Steps to Experiencing Happiness

Once more time: you cannot manufacture happiness—but you can prepare the soil for happiness to grow. Researchers have found the following seven qualifications in their studies of happy people.

1. **Be totally engaged.** An excessive separation between your private life and working life is an impediment to happiness. An "employee mentality" ("At 5:00, I drop my pen") hinders the flow. To experience happiness, you need to be ready to give yourself to something completely. People whose working life and personal life are integrated find it easier to experience flow.

2. **Concentrate on the moment.** Working only for the sake of achieving a distant goal (earning a lot of money, reaching a particular position) is detrimental to happiness. People experience flow when they are totally in the present moment. Time becomes irrelevant in the flow. All actions happen in the appropriate time, without haste but also without interruption. Time seems to stand still; the present moment seems timeless. Try to avoid comparisons with the past and dreams about the future. That way you have a greater chance of experiencing intense flow.

3. **Concentrate on one activity.** People who have to devote their attention to several activities at once are unable to get into the flow. You will be able to experience those moments of happiness only when you engage in an activity with your whole being.

4. **Learn to enjoy your work.** People who experience flow have managed to turn the restrictions of their working environment into opportunities. They see themselves as the criterion for their quality. Recognition from others or money they earn recede into the background. Among the people who Csikszentmihalyi discovered to be experiencing the greatest degree of happiness, there was a very simple worker in a steel mill who was popular with everyone on account of his specialized knowledge and willingness to help.

5. **Avoid working with unhappy colleagues.** Your working environ-

ment has a major influence on your experience of happiness. If you are surrounded by staff who grumble and have a negative attitude, it will be much more difficult for you to experience flow than it would be on a harmonious team. Identify clearly which people in your working environment suffer from chronic unhappiness and might infect you with it on an unconscious level. Keep a greater distance from those people or ask for a transfer.

6. **Look for a job where you have some control.** People who feel like victims and don't live but "are lived" lose their ability to enjoy themselves even if their work is exemplary. So change your job, even if the new one doesn't pay as well or is less prestigious. People who find happiness in their work will work so well that sooner or later they will profit, even on the level of money and prestige.

7. **Structure your free time.** Astonishingly, work is easier to enjoy than free time. Working life includes goals, rules, and challenges. On the

other hand, free time is unstructured and it takes effort to organize it in such a way as to make it enjoyable. So don't be reluctant to plan your free time and structure it deliberately. People who don't waste their free time have a more positive awareness of life; they live longer and they are less often sick. However, people who spend their time at work looking forward eagerly to going home and to the weekend seldom experience flow. Only 18% of all those questioned by Csikszentmihalyi experienced flow in the context of free time, and in almost all cases where they did, it was in the context of an organized hobby.

Simplifying Idea 17: Take the Strain out of Physical Fitness

95% of people who do sports in their spare time overdo it without realizing it. Sports are not automatically healthy—either for the body or for the mind. In almost all types of sports, even fitness training, there is a sort of class system: beginners, advanced athletes, and professionals. The person who bravely enters into a sport is initially humiliated. He or she doesn't want to be the worst in the group—and then he or she is already drawn into the need to compete, even if this is the very thing the person wanted to get away from through the sport.

So, should we not engage in sports? People sometimes quote Winston Churchill's philosophy: "First of all—no sports." People who go along with that should remember that the great cynic spent the last 14 years of his life in a wheelchair.

The solution is *enjoyment*! Gert von Kunhardt, the health coach and former professional athlete, said that in sports enjoyment should be compulsory: they should be fun instead of grueling, gentle movement instead of hard training.

Train for a Matter of Minutes

Back pain, tension, susceptibility to colds—you can avoid all that and more by working your muscles. Almost all the substances that the body needs in order to live and remain healthy can be produced in the muscles. Power and stamina training are indispensable for health and well-being. However, once they make a resolution to exercise, people almost always go too far. The advice for simplification: switch over to a homeopathic approach to exercise, in which small doses are sufficient.

The fastest method of getting atrophied muscles to grow again is to do *isometric exercises*: five to 10 seconds exerting your strength against an immovable object. *Balancing exercises* are good for the micro-muscular system and any dynamic exercise is good for the circulation. You can make this type of quick training a fixed part of your daily routine. The trick for simplification is to connect recurring activities with particular exercises:

- When you brush your teeth, get into a downhill skiing position and then gently bob up and down.
- After a shower, dry yourself with exaggerated, vigorous movements.

- When you shave, always do it standing on one leg.
- Even actions like buttoning up a shirt or blouse, putting on a tie on, putting on jewelry, tying shoelaces—all these things can be done standing on one leg.
- When you're walking and you have to wait, walk in place.
- When you're driving and you're waiting in traffic, push against the steering wheel for 10 seconds, tense your buttock muscles, and make circular movements with your head and shoulders.

Run with Awareness

Running is still one of the most efficient forms of exercise. But don't take marathon runners or student athletes as models; just think of yourself and follow Von Kunhardt's simple rules:

1. Warm up before you run: stretch and relax. One to two minutes are enough.

2. Consciously relax your arms and shoulders during the first 30 seconds when you run; avoid straining yourself and try to find a rhythm.

3. During the next minute of running, you should consciously apply the brakes—until you have the feeling of running in place.

4. During the next few minutes, you will be able to experience the fantastic processes in your body: the number of red blood corpuscles increases, blood pressure rises, blood vessels expand, and hormone regulation comes into operation.

5. Reduce your speed. Running should not be about achieving your best speed or setting a record; the important thing is just your own well-being. Don't worry if anyone gives you a sarcastic look. Forget all about the ideal sporty appearance of jogging. What you are doing is basic healthy jogging.

6. After five minutes, the body's adaptation processes will be complete. Now you can simply continue running. Enjoy your surroundings, the sky, the plants, and the smells and sounds of nature.

7. When you have been jogging for 10 to 20 minutes, there will be a qualitative leap: new capillaries develop, harmful cholesterol is broken down, and hormone balance adjusts to stress-reducing regulation. Subjectively, you have a feeling of lightness, a sense that you could go on running forever. If you come to a "dead end," you have done something wrong.

If you prefer biking, just apply the same rules. The healthiest bicycle for the back and joints is the good old simple one-speed bicycle or touring bicycle, where you sit with the upper body as upright as possible.

Use Walking as a Source of Strength

It doesn't always have to be running in jogging gear. If you want to relax and at the same time train the most important sets of muscles in your body, go for a walk. Normal walking in the open air is particularly good for improving your general fitness, reducing the risk of heart disease, and keeping your weight under control.

The many positive effects do not come about overnight. It's best to make walking part of your daily routine. (That's why it's so good to have a dog that has to be taken out every day, no matter what the weather.)

Start with 30 minutes each day, regardless of the weather. And remember the words of Scottish comedian Billy Connolly: "There's no such thing as bad weather, just the wrong clothing." Don't just stroll;

walk with a sense of purpose but without haste. There will only be a marginal increase in your pulse when you walk; the increase will be much less than with jogging.

Find a partner: your spouse, a friend, a child, or a dog, perhaps the neighbor's dog.

Count your steps and breathe consciously at the same time: breathe in for six steps, hold your breath for six steps, breathe out for six steps, and take six steps before breathing in again. Then do the whole cycle again. If six steps are too much for you, change the number to suit yourself. This breathing exercise, which comes from India, will help to develop a calm, balanced state of mind. It also helps the mind to become clear and receptive.

Find a destination for your daily walk: a particular tree, a lake, a river, a place with a nice view—a pleasant place of some sort where you like to be. Notice how it changes over the seasons. This turns the walk into a "little pilgrimage" and you will get more mental energy. One very good idea comes from Johann Wolfgang von Goethe. He always took violet seeds with him when he went for a walk. (They won't cost much if you buy them in a market.) He scattered them along the wayside and he liked to watch the flowers come up the following year where he had been walking.

Motivation Aids

- Start with a little exercise: it should be refreshing rather than exhausting! Do less than you are able to do.
- Start because you're convinced, not because you're persuaded.
- Make a training plan. When to begin? How often? For how long? Where?
- Get someone to check what you're doing: arrange to meet up with a training partner (but not someone who will expect too much of you!); record each completed training session on a calendar.

- Be clear with yourself that even five minutes of training session is a gain.
- Make use of every stairway and every other opportunity to get some exercise.
- It's never too late! Astonishing muscle growth and cardiovascular improvement is possible even at the age of 70.

Simplifying Idea 18: Purify Your Body

Get rid of those excess pounds—but not through dieting or special slimming programs. The simplification principle is as follows: regular instead of excessive, evolution instead of revolution, small steps instead of dramatic action. You can take nine simple steps to rearrange your everyday life in such a way that you achieve a normal, healthy weight in one to two years without any strenuous effort.

If you use the right method, you will actually find it easier to lose weight than to remain overweight. Nothing has such a simplifying effect on life as feeling good in your body and radiating physical fitness, inwardly and outwardly.

1. Paint a Perfect Portrait

Very few people think they look perfect: stomach too big, nose too long, teeth too yellow, forehead too high, breasts too big or too small, bad skin or wrinkles.... In the worst case, you might concentrate so much on your imperfections that you have no energy to do anything about the aspects of your appearance that can be changed (e.g., obesity).

The idea for simplification is to do things the other way around. Stand in front of the mirror and say what you like about yourself: it might be your eyes, your hands, your smile, or your voice. You will be amazed what a positive effect this exercise can have; when it comes to fitness and eating sensibly, this exercise is a more powerful motivator than constantly finding fault.

Then picture yourself standing naked in front of the mirror feeling very content with your appearance. Imagine it as vividly as you can. The basis for this exercise is the fact that we store inner models in the right side of the brain, which is responsible for unified concepts, feelings, and images. This side of the brain has a strong connection with the subconscious. In the long run, the positive image will have an effect and you will develop in accordance with that positive effect.

Don't generate any negative images or ideas ("I am too fat," "Oh God, look at me!"), because these messages lodge in your subconscious. Say positive things instead: "My body is getting rid of its fat reserves," "I look better every day," or similar things.

Talk about your slimming program in positive terms. Remember that you can think of physical exercise, exertion, or healthy eating in terms of being good to yourself.

2. Weigh Yourself Every Morning

Even if the goal of your slimming program cannot be defined as a number of pounds, you won't get anywhere without the scales. You need an absolutely regular daily check. You always have to monitor your weight trends: is it rising or declining? A great system is to post a sheet of paper on the wall where *you and your partner* write down your weights every day. If you see the figures going up after a feast, you can both take countermeasures.

3. Eat Only Fruit for Breakfast

You don't have to reduce your food intake drastically in order to reduce your weight; you just have to change the type of food. After the short time it takes to get used to it, you will find it easy to prepare a varied breakfast with just fruit. Pineapple is particularly good for stimulating the metabolism. (But don't eat just pineapple; otherwise, you'll have too much acid in your stomach.) The best option is a tasty mixture of various fruits. You don't need to worry about the quantity. Eat until you feel full. Eating fruit for breakfast has a further positive effect. Eating nothing but fruit before 11:00 a.m. is a natural way of cleansing the bowels—a fountain of youth for the whole body.

4. Eat Life

Look at each element of your food and ask yourself: is it alive or dead? By nature, we eat only things that are fresh. That is why dead things have to be seasoned and prepared to make them taste nice. Live things include fruit and vegetables and grain if it has not been overprocessed. They contain the truly valuable resources of our food: vitamins and trace elements. Dead foods include meat, most types of fat, refined sugar, and all sorts of canned foods and junk food (chips, spicy sausage, French fries, chocolate …).

5. Eat at Lunch According to Your Appetite

Like all animals, humans have a clear measure for limiting their food intake: when you've had enough, the food ceases to be appetizing. We still have this instinct, but we tend to trick it, perhaps with refined preparation or social pressures ("Come and have something to eat," "Eat everything on your plate!").

After observing yourself carefully for a few days, you will soon find a point when you are full and don't want any more. You should then enjoy the feeling of being satisfied and not worry about leaving the rest on your plate. Keep to regular eating times as much as possible. Your body will get used to it, it will process food better, and your feeling of hunger will diminish.

6. Eat Less in the Evening

Digesting food in the evening is particularly strenuous for the body; most of the accumulation of fat is caused by eating in the evening. An evening meal is the easiest one to skip and it makes the biggest difference on the scales. Two meals are enough (breakfast and a moderate lunch).

However, in many families gathering for supper is an important social event. That's fine: have a small salad, a tomato, pickles, a piece of crispbread, or something else that is very low in calories. That will be OK.

7. Indulge Yourself with Pleasure

You don't have to decline invitations to dinners or even banquets. The body can easily cope with a burst of calories when you've adjusted to less food. It then automatically almost fasts the next day.

8. Relax

Most diets fail because people concentrate much too much on their stomachs. (When I tried the "Hollywood Diet," I kept dreaming of but-tered pretzels.) People either put on weight after the diet (yo-yo effect) or give up and go back to their old bad habits.

It's smarter to change your eating bit by bit. Do it gradually so that your partner or your family can do it with you. It's much harder to do it alone. You will feel better with each step. You will enjoy the simple life *immediately*—you don't have to wait for some far-off time when you have reached your ideal.

9. Drink Water

When you feel hungry between meals, no yogurt, cookies, chocolate bars, or cake: just drink water. Try various brands until you find your favorite water. The best thing is to have a large glass of water *before* eating. Then you'll eat less than you normally do. Don't be persuaded by advice to eat lots of small meals; at the end of the day, you will have eaten more than you intended.

Drink as little coffee and black tea as possible. You will feel tired for a few days. But soon after this "detoxification" stage, you will be amazed how wide awake you feel without the ups and downs caused by stimulants.

The Iranian-American doctor, Fereydoon Batmanghelidj, summa-rizes the result of his years of research in one statement: most of the illnesses found in modern society are not the result of faulty metabolism but the body's thirst signals. The situation is paradoxical: even though we take in enormous quantities of liquids, our bodies suffer from dehydration. The reason is that most of our drinks have disastrous side effects.

Why You Don't Lose Weight with Artificially Sweetened Drinks

Batmanghelidj found in his practice that the patients who gained a lot of weight were the ones who drank diet drinks exclusively. The reason is that over 80% of what people drink in the U.S. contains caffeine. It is a drug that has a direct effect on the brain and can induce all the symptoms of addiction. It also stimulates the kidneys and causes dehydration. That's the reason why people drink so much cola: the water does not remain in the body for long; this is noticeable as people feel the need to urinate very soon after drinking coffee or cola. At the same time, people misinterpret their thirst for water. Since they believe they have already drunk enough, they think they must be hungry. Consequently, they eat more than their bodies need.

The secret is adenosine triphosphate (ATP), a chemical compound in the brain that ensures the release of stored energy. Caffeine seems to lower the reaction threshold for the ATP storage: the energy reserves in the brain cells are activated and you feel in better condition. Cola that contains sugar does at least to some extent satisfy the brain's need for energy and it replenishes part of the reserves that have been used. Artificially sweetened drinks do not do that. The result is an increased feeling of hunger and thirst.

The body knows from experience that it gets energy when you drink something that tastes sweet. The liver adapts for the intake of sugar and reduces the conversion of the body's protein and starch reserves. If this adaptation is not followed by real sugar, the liver sends a message to the brain: "Hunger!" Series of experiments have proved repeatedly that the feeling of hunger caused by sweeteners can last up to 90 minutes—even if the body has already had enough food. People who go without drinks containing sugar for dietary reasons eat more than their bodies need.

Why You Shouldn't Go Without Salt in Your Food

Many diets bring about rapid weight loss by banishing salt completely. This is a dangerous trick, because the "success" of the diet consists merely of a lack of water. If the body gets too little salt for a sustained  period, you get acid in some of the cells, which damages the DNA structure and can cause cancer. Salt deficiency may also be one of the primary reasons for the increasing incidence of osteoporosis.

Salt and water are also of critical importance for asthma and allergies. They both reduce the production of the neurotransmitter histamine, to which most allergic reactions are attributed. Nowadays, salt in food is commonly regarded as something negative, although it is in fact a natural antihistamine that is needed in the lungs to keep the airways moist and to dissolve mucus.

The Right Way to Drink

A rule of thumb: drink a glass of water (eight ounces) half an hour before eating (breakfast, lunch, dinner) and about the same amount two and a half hours after each meal. That is the minimum. To make sure the body gets what it needs, you should drink two glasses of water with your main meal and one before going to bed.

Just water. Ordinary tap water is best. If it is chlorinated, let it stand in an open jug; after a while the chlorine evaporates and the smell disappears. Because of their dehydrating effect, alcohol, coffee, black tea, and  other drinks containing caffeine do not count as water!

You can calculate your minimum daily requirement more precisely: a little under a half ounce of water per pound of body weight: if you weigh 130 pounds, you will need about 60 ounces; if you weigh 175 pounds, you will need about 80 ounces. If you drink this much pure water, you won't feel the urge to drink more water. You won't find your-self indulging in evening excesses of beer and wine.

A cup of motivation. Put a really big glass of water where you work, preferably a 16-ounce glass—or beer mug. It will soon become a good habit to take a drink regularly and thereby prevent any raven-ous hunger for candies or other evils.

Warm in the winter. When it's cold outside, you should replace the large glass with a thermos jug with just hot water. This is one of the most amazing recipes for simplification: after just one week, a cup of hot water will make you as wide awake as a cup of coffee or tea used to make you. Hot water is also very helpful if you are hoarse or if you are coming down with a cold—it's a standard proven remedy from the Ayurvedic medicine of India.

Put salt on food. Make sure you increase your salt intake when you drink more water. When you drink a quart of water, your body needs about a quarter or a third teaspoon of salt. (You'll know if you're getting too much salt, because your body will swell.) Signs of salt deficiency are muscle cramps at night, cramps in muscles that you haven't been train-ing, and feelings of dizziness.

Batmanghelidj found that water is the cheapest medicine for a dehydrated body. Regular adequate water intake prevents many dis-eases and disorders that people worry about, such as diabetes, heart dis-ease, gastric ulcers, intestinal ulcers, chronic sinusitis, and many others that are frequently associated with emotional difficulties.

Healthy Sleep with Water and Salt

With patients who couldn't sleep, Batmanghelidj had very good results with the following simple remedy. Drink a glass of water before going to bed and then put a bit of salt on your tongue. Let your tongue relax and don't press it against the roof of your mouth. This combination changes the strength of the electrical discharge in the brain and helps you go to sleep.

The Speaker and His Glass of Water

If you have to give a speech now and then, use this simplification trick: whenever you lose your train of thought during your talk, stop speaking for a few seconds and reach for a glass of water next to the lectern. We don't know the reason, but a sip of clear water makes your thoughts clear as well. More than 90% of the time, you'll find your way back to the subject after drinking a little water. (If it doesn't work, just ask the audience, "Where was I?" No one will hold it against you.) That's why you should always pour yourself a glass of water before you give a talk, even if you are not thirsty.

Simplifying Idea 19: The Best Way to Relax

Our society is tired. Adults now sleep more than 70 minutes less each day than their grandparents. For children and young people, the difference in relation to people of the same age in the year 1910 is actually 90 minutes. Nowadays, a lot of problems with the immune system, infections, diseases of the nervous system, migraines, and allergies have one simple cause: too little sleep.

Scientists believe that the major function of sleep is to recharge the brain's depleted batteries. Mental reserves are mobilized and mood improves; sleep also improves the ability to react and to be productive.

American sleep researcher John M. Taub of the University of Virginia was able to prove this already in 1976 in a prominent study. His subject sleepers were 15% more quick-witted after each nap, they made one third fewer errors, their mood was better, and they were less anxious and exhausted. Their energy levels rose noticeably.

It is a medically proven fact that it is unhealthy to sleep much too little or much too much. Having less than four hours or more than 10 hours sleep is dangerous to health, according to tests conducted by Berlin sleep researcher Karl Hecht; it doubles your mortality risk! Apart from this, you can work out your own optimum sleep pattern, which can include sleeping at night and napping at various times during the day. This may involve breaking away from old habits.

The Simplifying Micro-Sleep Method

Here are the best sleep tips for optimum deep relaxation.

Napoleon's Rule for Sleep

Four hours for men, five for women, and six for idiots: this was Napoleon's tough sleep regime. He managed with very little sleep at night, but he made up for it with several short periods of sleep throughout the day. The important factor in compensating for sleep deficit is not so much how long you sleep but how often you go to sleep. It is presumed that, at the moment we begin falling asleep, the body produces growth hormones that facilitate powerful recuperation.

The Da Vinci Formula

It is said that the genius of the Italian Renaissance, Leonardo da Vinci, didn't sleep at all at night during stressful phases and times when he was engaged in creative work. Instead, he took a 15-minute nap every four hours.

Sleep researcher Claudio Stampi of Harvard University discovered that people could remain really productive with this method over a limited period of time. People who race sailboats make use of the idea. The most effective way is to have three 25- to 30-minute periods of sleep and a 90-minute "anchor sleep" (which lets your body know that it's night).

No-Go Periods and Windows for Healthy Sleep

Every day there are two no-go periods when it's particularly difficult to go to sleep. They are between 10:00 a.m. and 11:00 a.m. and between 8:00 p.m. and 9:00 p.m. You should not sleep during these active phrases.

Every 90 minutes, a sort of time window opens in the brain: this is just the right entry point for a short refreshing sleep. The entry point is  very easy to find: when you feel most tired is the best time for a nap.

When the sleep window opens, your body reacts. You feel tired, you yawn, your eyelids start drooping, your head feels heavy, and your reflexes slow down. You rub your eyes, you rest your head in your hands, you feel listless and unfocused, and your thoughts wander. If you get a nap at this point, you will be living with your body rather than against it. The result: you will be altogether fresher and more energetic.

Work out Your Sleep Requirement

Take a test. You're suffering from real sleep deficiency if the following apply:

- You lie down during the day and doze off in less than 10 minutes (even less time in the case of teenagers and young adults).
- You nod off in the train or on the bus.
- During meetings or presentations you suddenly notice that you've missed the last few sentences.

Here is the remedy for lack of sleep. Make it a regular practice to get at least seven hours of sleep each night and a nap in the afternoon when possible. If necessary, you can make up for a large sleep deficit on the weekend. One thing that does not work is to get more sleep in advance, to "bank sleep." If there's a period when you don't sleep enough, the body can easily make up for it by getting eight hours of sleep each night for two or three days. Don't try to compensate for a period when you sleep much too little by sleeping a lot; that can cause depression and apathy.

The Best Tips for Your Naps

1. A positive approach. Stand by your policy of getting a short sleep without feeling guilty. The more positive your attitude, the more effective your sleep will be in making you healthy. If your manager or colleagues don't want to allow it, you can explain, "People who take a regular after-lunch nap take fewer days off sick. A midday nap accords with the human biorhythm." A long-term study carried out by the medical faculty of the University of Athens showed clearly that having a sleep at midday reduces the risk of cardiac infarction by 30%. Companies such as SAP and Siemens have set up rest zones for staff, which has led to a clear increase in productivity.

2. **Regularity.** If possible, try to take your nap at the same time under the same conditions each day. It's best to sleep in the afternoon between 2:00 and 5:00 for at least four minutes. When people sleep during this period, they get more than twice the benefit of recuperative deep sleep as they do when they sleep at other times of the day. If you have no opportunity at work, you may be able to take a short sleep after work, before your leisure activities.

3. **A fixed ritual.** Make use of associations that help you to go to sleep: the same armchair, a small cushion. Turn off the telephone, loosen your clothing, make a few movements to relax the muscles, and read a meditative text. Find out what works for you personally.

4. **A pleasant room.** Sleep in a familiar room that you find calming and reassuring. It should be quiet, slightly darkened, and not too warm—about 60° to 65° F.

5. **Quality, not quantity.** The recuperative effect of a nap is determined more by the right time than by the overall duration. A very short sleep that begins at the optimum time (when a sleep window opens) has as much of a rejuvenating effect as a protracted siesta, if not more. As a rule, four to 20 minutes is the optimum.

6. **You can sleep anywhere.** Sit in the so-called "coachman's position" with your legs spread apart on a stool. Lean your head and upper body slightly forward and rest your hands and forearms on your thighs and knees.

In waiting rooms, on train rides, and similar situations, sit with your back upright, well supported, with your head inclined forwards or backwards. An important point for the circulation: don't cross your legs.

If you're sitting at a desk, lay your hands and elbows flat on the surface and rest your head on your arms.

An alternative is to use a briefcase (provided it's flat and not too hard) or a folded pullover sweater or jacket as a cushion; put it on the desk, place your arms around it, and then rest your head on it.

7. **Listen until you are tired.** Listen to meditative music or the sound of a fan or an air-conditioning system. The more even and predictable the sequence of notes or noises, the easier it will be to go to sleep. Or you can imagine you are lying in a hut on the Fiji Islands in the Pacific Ocean listening to the gentle sound of the sea with crickets chirping in the background.

8. **Eating can make you tired.** Meals containing carbohydrates help you to fall asleep and they make the sleep last longer: a piece of bread or a roll, potatoes, a bit of candy, a glass of milk. Don't drink large quantities of liquid before going to sleep.

9. **Waking up right.** Don't get up abruptly. A rule of thumb: allow as

much time to wake up as for falling asleep. Help your body to wake up by breathing in and out consciously. Stretching and yawning help you to wake up. Splashing cold water on your face (good for low blood pressure), brushing your teeth, a glass of cold water, and a light meal containing protein (e.g., yogurt) cause the brain to give out stimulating neurotransmitters.

10. **Are you firmly opposed to naps?** Some people feel washed out after a short sleep, which is why they would rather not do it. But even they can benefit from a short period of sleep. As a rule, it doesn't

take more than four or five days to change over from being dead set against midday siestas to becoming a nap enthusiast. It is particularly worthwhile to make the adjustment when you notice that you are getting older and that your general productivity is decreasing. Particularly tough cases need 20 days to get used to the new habit. After this phase, you will feel fit and your mood will be positive after a short sleep, if you manage to integrate the habit into your daily routine.

Take the Grumpiness out of the Morning

Only 8% of us are distinctly night people who are no good in the morning. A joint study conducted by English and American universities over a long period of time showed that the overwhelming majority of people are flexible, mixed types. In other words, most people who are grumpy in the morning are not especially like that by nature; they have just told themselves they are over and over again until they believe it. So almost anyone can get over the morning blues—provided they know how.

Something warm before you get up. The body loses one to two quarts of water during the night. The sooner you make up for this loss, the better. Ideally, you should drink two glasses of mineral water on an empty stomach. Or, if you prefer something warm, put a thermos flask with warm tea or hot broth next to the bed in the evening and drink some in the morning before you get out of bed.

Stretching. Learn from dogs and cats. After eight hours of sleep, your muscles, ligaments, and tendons will have contracted slightly. If you have a good stretch while you're still in bed (whatever works for you, naturally), you give your body a signal: increase the oxygen supply, release the hormones that produce happiness, prepare the muscles for action. Take five minutes for this process.

When pregnant women are very tired, midwives advise them to raise their arms, stretch their fingers out, make a fist, vigorously stretch out their fingers again, repeating the whole procedure 10 times. This pumping exercise with the hands gets the circulation going, rather like warming up a diesel engine.

Aromatherapy. Put your favorite perfume or cologne on the bedside table. As soon as the alarm clock rings, put a bit of it on the back of your hand and smell the frangrance of the day. It works for both women and men. You can try it with scented oils. The following have a stimulating effect: chamomile, lavender, peppermint, rosemary, juniper, and lemon.

Get going with gratitude. American writer Henry David Thoreau asked

himself the same three questions each morning when he woke up: What is good in my life? What can I be happy about? What should I be thankful for? The answers to these questions tend to engender a friendly, positive, and active state of mind.

Clearing the way. American doctor and psychologist Reid Wilson points out that a depressive mood in the morning may be due to an unconscious aversion to the small details of the morning routine. You might also have negative expectations about what the day will bring. Do a very honest analysis: What gets on your nerves in the morning? In particular, who? Do you need more peace? If necessary, get up earlier so that you have time for yourself.

Time is still the most important ingredient for a successful morning schedule. People who begin the morning already under the control of the second hand of the clock put their body and soul into the "Faster! Faster!" mode. Allow an extra half hour for your normal routine. Take time for yourself. Enjoy your bathroom routines. When the weather is good, sit outside on a balcony or terrace enjoy breakfast without hurrying. You will then find that the morning turns into a source of relaxation and happiness.

Preparing for the morning. Optimize your "launching pad": get your clothes and work things ready the night before and prepare the breakfast table.

A tidy, well-lit, clean bathroom with a nice smell is important for a good start to the day. There should be at least one thing you look forward to in the bathroom: a radio tuned to your favorite station, flowers, towels warmed on the radiator, etc.

Water on the outside. A shower has an invigorating effect only if the warm shower is followed by cold water (60° F). The best way to use a cold jet of water is the method explained by Sebastian Kneipp, a 19th-century priest and hydrotherapist. Gradually bring the cold closer to the heart area: first the right leg, then the right arm, then the left leg, the left arm, the back, and the chest. The shock effect is noticeably less if you hold cold water in your mouth at the same time.

Getting the newspaper is good medicine. A real simplifying tip: if you go out in the morning to get the newspaper, put on a coat and make the trip to the front porch, the mailbox, or the driveway into a three-minute walk. Fresh air before the first meal gets your circulation and metabolism going.

A good mood with green tea. Extensive tests were carried out by sports doctors at the University of Chicago on breakfast beverages; the best choice was clearly shown to be green tea. It removes less water from your body than black tea or coffee. (The latter also causes too much acidity in the body.) Green tea also increases the level of serotonin, which has a positive effect on mood.

You've now taken a few more steps along the path of simplification. Your consciousness is now more able to deal with the many simplifications and improvements that make up the great way to your inner goal. You are now ready to incorporate a further dimension of your life into the way of simplification: the people around you.

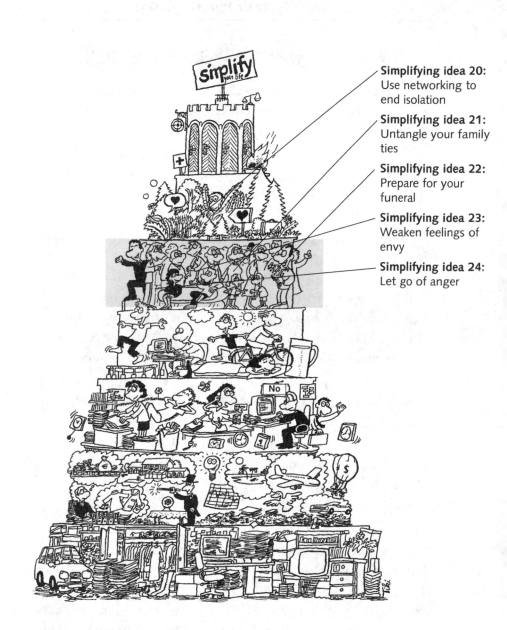

Simplifying idea 20:
Use networking to end isolation

Simplifying idea 21:
Untangle your family ties

Simplifying idea 22:
Prepare for your funeral

Simplifying idea 23:
Weaken feelings of envy

Simplifying idea 24:
Let go of anger

Step 5 of Your Life Pyramid:
Simplify Your Relationships

Your Dream of Simplicity: Sixth Night

Now that you have left the mirrors, bars, and conduits from the previous level of your life pyramid behind you, you consciously look down to the foot of the pyramid for the first time. You feel a certain pride when you see the size of the edifice that represents your life. At the same time, you are surprised how empty the levels below you seem now. You become aware how alone you were on the first four levels.

As you look around you, you have to laugh as you see where this feeling comes from. The places behind you and next to you are teeming with people. People greet you with a loud "Hello!" and friends pat you on the shoulder. It's a happy reunion with people you'd almost forgotten and, as they embrace you and ask about what's been going on in your life, you notice further acquaintances silently waiting for you in the background.

Your life consists of more than just your own life. Many thousands of other lives are interconnected with your life. You would have expected this level to be somewhat smaller; in fact, you're no longer even sure whether this pyramid really is shaped like a pyramid, because it sometimes seems as though the levels get bigger you ascend.

You see your parents and your grandparents and, in the distant haze, you think you even catch a glimpse of their parents. A great many people involved in your life are no longer alive, but on this level, which seems so gigantic, there is no longer even a distinction between life and death. Class differences also become insignificant. You see your old managers and teachers as well as people who were dependent on you. You see people who are grateful to you and people to whom you are still indebted. You see your children—and perhaps children you could have had. Sometimes you think you even can see children whom you could still have.

You see people you've loved, although the relationships have ended. You sense that in some particular way you're still connected with them. The one person you don't see is your current partner. But then you look up and see that your partner is patiently waiting for you on the next level. You plunge into the bustle of the fifth story of your life pyramid.

Simplifying Objective for Step 5

Learn to maintain, deepen, and enjoy relationships with other people with mutual giving and receiving.

Do you know that wonderful feeling when problems just evaporate into thin air as you talk them over with someone else? When you get help that you didn't expect? Or when you are able to do something good for someone else? A life without such relationships is poor and complicated. On the other hand, a life with friends and acquaintances is rich and simple. Many of the simplification methods we have looked at so far are much more effective when you try them out and practice them with other people.

This chapter tells you how to find those people.

Simplifying Idea 20:
Use Networking to End Isolation

If you read the gossip columns in lifestyle magazines, you will see how often prominent people meet up with other prominent people. That is the secret for building up a network: it's through these meetings that prominent people become prominent in the first place! You might write a bestseller, make a fantastic appearance on television, hold seminars that are so good they become legendary, or have incredible success in business, but if you are isolated in your private life afterwards, your success will be just a flash in the pan.

Nobody gets anywhere in a profession without networking. People used to call it "connections" in a disparaging way. Over the years, it has become a generally recognized method because it helps everyone concerned. We should not regard networking as a search for customers or protégés, but rather as a win-win situation from which everyone can benefit.

It's not WHAT you know, it's WHO you know.

Networking must not be a obstinate quest: "Will this person be any use to me?" Trust your innate feelings of antipathy and sympathy. If you like someone, invest time in your relationship with him or her, regardless of whether it is a colleague or a fleeting acquaintance. Enjoy relationships with customers and colleagues whom you appreciate. At the same time, think in both directions—not just "What can this person do to help me get somewhere?" but also "How can I help the other person so that he or she will want to network with me?"

Basic rule 1: Stick to it in the beginning. If you hardly ever speak to a new colleague for three months, it will be difficult to become buddies with him in the fourth month.

Basic rule 2: Don't push. Give the other person the opportunity to approach you. Move closer, step by step.

Basic rule 3: Don't leave everything to chance. Even though friendly relations are in the end a gift, it is worth planning social contacts. Here are some tried and tested things to help you.

Set "Visiting Hours"

Simplify the increasingly troublesome issue of making arrangements with colleagues, friends, and acquaintances who never have time. Choose a particular day each month for your house to be open to visitors (perhaps the evening of the first

Friday of every month). Don't set the standard too high when it comes to the food. Since you can never be quite sure how many guests will appear, you will constantly need to improvise—which gives the gathering a certain charm.

If that all seems too expensive or if that method seems to leave contacts too much to chance, here is an easier solution: decide on a specific day of the month on which you can invite guests specifically.

A Day for the Extended Family

You can do something similar with parents, grandparents, parents-in-law, brothers and sisters, uncles and aunts: suggest a family gathering once per year. That way people can see each other and renew connections even with distant relatives. This sort of reunion drastically reduces the number of individual visits by relatives  and it makes it easier for the family members who find it difficult to socialize.

Make It Easier to Form New Contacts

When you organize a party, a seminar, a family party, or whatever, make sure you don't just get the people who already know each other clustering together.

If you invite people to a meal, you can use place cards to facilitate successful networking. Organize games so that people sitting at each table can mix.

When you announce, "The buffet is open," address the subject openly by saying, "Take this opportunity to get to know new people." A lot of people find this a sufficiently effective icebreaker to be able to start speaking to others.

Don't be afraid of issuing name badges at large gatherings if people don't know each other. Get each person to write something typical but a bit mysterious on the badge. That is a really nice way of making it possible for people to start a conversation with people they don't know.

Combine Cooking and Networking

Think about which of your friends you could do some cooking with.

You can then arrange a meal that includes preparing the food together. Then you won't be working away alone under stress in the kitchen; you will get twice as much done in the same time—and you will learn a few extra culinary tricks as well. If you prepare so much food that you keep some of it, which you can use the next day or the following, the time-saving effect will be even greater.

The Kindness Chain

Oprah Winfrey, the uncrowned queen of American TV chat shows, created something that has had an effect on American society for more than five years now. It's called the "kindness chain." Every viewer is

supposed to do something good for another person—preferably someone who won't be expecting it: give something (flowers, a book, a CD, or something else), pay a visit, do some shopping for the person, invite him or her to dinner, or some other nice idea. The more imaginative, the better. There is only one condition: the recipient is not allowed to reciprocate; instead he or she is supposed to do something for another person. And so it continues. It has led to the most wonderful things: from florists who are amazed at completely new customers to hostile neighbors who suddenly become good friends. The good thing about this idea is that it can be done in any country. You don't need a TV talk-show host to start doing it yourself.

How to Get Invited to Interesting Events

The person responsible for invitation lists for celebrations or parties in large companies is usually the director's secretary or the PR department. Find out who is responsible and say quite openly, "I would really like to come to the celebration during the trade fair." As a rule the organizers are pleased when people show an interest: there are usually more than enough people who have to be there or who are there unwillingly.

At the celebration, go up to the people who arranged your invitation and thank them. If people like you, you will soon be on the next guest list.

The Way to Behave at a Party

Don't just leave things to chance; set objectives. "I would like to speak to Professor Bighead for at least five minutes and he should then remember my name." Or "I want to at last get to know Rita outside of the stressful office environment so that we can get over the tensions between us."

But don't let these objectives keep you from being open to surprise encounters. Each time you meet someone, regard it primarily as a game and as something relaxing, not as a continuation of work by different means.

Make sure you keep a balance between "sending" and "receiving." Listen and contribute to the conversation. Take an interest in the other person without interrogating him or her. Tell things about yourself that you would also be interested to know about the other person. It's helpful to have something that works as a "conversation piece" to get things going: an unusual tie, an original pin. Sometimes a stylish new pair of shoes will do the trick.

Don't worry about starting a conversation with something quite banal: say something nice about the buffet or talk about the weather. The main thing is that your conversation should not remain on this opening topic.

How to Become a Welcome Guest

You find the most important contacts in private and professional life when you get invitations from other people. It can lead to valuable friendships, but also to lasting animosities—and the latter can be caused merely by a little carelessness. Put yourself in the position of your hosts and ask yourself what you, in their position, would expect from the guests.

Acknowledge the Invitation

If you get a written invitation, it's always good to confirm that you are going to come, even if it's not expressly requested. "RSVP" is a polite way of saying, "Hey, help me plan! Then I've got to order food and borrow some chairs!"

Bring Some Flowers

A bunch of cut flowers (not potted plants) is the safest small present. It  does, however, mean extra stress for the host: getting rid of the paper, finding a vase, cutting the stems, and arranging the flowers. That's why ready-made flower arrangements in a bowl with a floral sponge are so popular—a simplifying idea for the guest and host. If the sponge is kept moist regularly, the flowers last at least as long as conventional cut flowers. At the same time, consider avoiding:

- carnations (a lot of people regard them as cheap and unoriginal)
- red roses, which may be seen as a declaration of love
- lilies, gladioli, and flowers that could be misunderstood as being the type of flowers people put on graves

You can also give a man flowers. A lot of places where single people live could do with a bit of color. If the host complains, "But you shouldn't have!" just take it as politeness and give him or her flowers again the next time.

Arrive Punctually

 The meaning of "punctually" varies according to the situation. For a party in a private home, it's best to arrive within eight minutes after the indicated time. However, if the invitation is for a meal, you should arrive promptly. If it's a cocktail party, it's generally OK to arrive a little

late—but no more than 30 minutes. If the invitation is for an "open house" and indicates a time range, it's best to arrive no later than an hour before the ending time. Finally, never arrive early, so you don't interrupt any final preparations.

Be Outgoing

It's quite demanding to have very reserved guests who always wait for the host to take the initiative. Make it easy on your host. If you don't know anyone at a party, speak to the person next to you. The simplest way to open a conversation is "What's your connection with the hosts?" That usually leads to other subjects very quickly. Don't spend the whole evening talking to one person.

When the host says it's time to eat, don't be shy about being the first one to the table. It used to be regarded as polite to be very reserved at that moment, but nowadays it's considered more negatively.

Help your host; approach guests who look shy and bring them into the conversation.

Don't Hold the Hosts Captive

You should definitely chat with the hosts, but don't monopolize them. Make sure that every guest can get a fair share of the hosts' attention. At big parties it's impossible for the hosts to approach every guest. You need to take the initiative.

Approach other people with a goal. Use every meeting for purposeful networking. If you want to meet a particular guest, ask your host to introduce you. Hosts will be pleased to do that, because their aim is to make sure that the guests make contact with each other.

Observe Taboos

In any country there will be subjects that you need to avoid in order to avoid offending guests and hosts. Don't make any disparaging remarks about the food you are offered ("Didn't you know that pork is very bad for you?") or about other guests. Moralistic lectures by vegetarians next to a buffet with roast beef are likewise simply impolite, no matter how convinced you may be of your dietary policies. Don't blurt things out about politics, religion, money, or illnesses. Whatever you do, don't educate other people's children.

Say Good Things About the Food

But be quite honest. If you find the delicacies horrible, say something nice about the wine. At the buffet, start by putting a bit of everything on your plate, to find out which things you like. Make sure to keep yourself completely under control. Never embarrass your host by drinking too much. Agree beforehand with the person accompanying you to the party that you will both leave quietly if one of you drinks too much. "Quietly" means especially not having a public discussion of the issue: "You've ad too much to drink again."

Leave at the Right Time

Disappearing too early is just as impolite as outstaying your welcome.

The simplest way is to follow the majority. Whatever you do, don't leave without saying goodbye and thanking the hosts sincerely. You should thank them again. In some circles, the custom is to phone the hosts the following day to thank them for the evening. It's a good opportunity to follow up contacts ("Who was that crazy pianist?") so that an encounter can develop into a friendly relationship.

Simplifying Idea 21:
Untangle Your Family Ties

It is the most difficult, complicated, and also the most important relationship in your life. Guilt, passion, anger, friendship, love, dependency—these are issues for every adult when it comes to relationships with his or her mother or father. There will be a large number of feelings, some of which will be in conflict with each other, that bind you to the people who brought you into the world—especially, of course, your mother. Some strong, grown-up people turn into quivering wrecks when their mothers come to visit.  There is hardly ever a session with a therapist in which the client's relationship with his or her parents is not discussed. And every year at Christmas the subject becomes more timely than ever.

Be aware of your parents' age. As a small child you saw your parents as "modern," as up-to-date. However, as an adult you need to keep in mind that your parents are a generation older than you. In most cases this means they will not be able to talk as openly about everything as you can. They will probably be living at a different speed than you. In view of the statistically high life expectancy of the older generation, these differences will probably increase. Allow for this.

Listen to your parents. You no longer have to obey your parents as you did when you were a child. But it is good to listen to them and keep as open as possible. Let them know that you understand their views even if you don't necessarily share them. Grown-up offspring sometimes tend to dictate to their parents and cut them short: "Yes, yes, you've said that a thousand times." These things are more hurtful to elderly people than they generally let on.

Your parents have experienced more than you. This point may seem trite, but it is often overlooked: your parents were alive before you were born. Let them tell you as much about their time as possible so that you can understand them. Remember your own youth  and from that standpoint ask them, "What was it like when you fell in love for the first time? How did your parents treat you? What did you do in your free time in those days?"

Ask your parents about the past. It's usually the mother who knows most about old times and elderly people frequently like to speak about them. Don't let them get away with some little generalized statement ("I had a hard childhood"). Ask them about actual stories and put new questions to them. Gather all the facts; it might seem like quite a bit of work at the moment, but it's one of the most valuable legacies that you can pass on to your children. It is often possible even if your relationship with your parents is emotionally strained.

Make life easier for your parents. A lot of adults rely on the natural unspoken understanding that they had with their parents when they were children. The result in later life is that they feel sure they can tell what their parents need just by looking at them—and they don't discover how untrue this is. The parents often do not dare to disagree.

Here's an example. The son invites his mother to go to the opera on her birthday because that was what she always wanted in the past; he's really surprised that she is then in a bad mood. The reason is that she actually hates opera and she took an interest in it only for the sake of her husband, who is now dead. A simple, open question would have solved the whole problem.

Get to know your parents' relatives. If you have not already done so, make contact with your parents' siblings and their other relatives and friends. Organize family get-togethers if nobody else does. If there is hostility among family members, try to bring about reconciliation as a representative of the younger generation—without adopting the role of peacemaker. Be active in the background; make sure there are opportunities for the people concerned to talk to each other. They then have to resolve it themselves. Ending old disputes is the best investment for your future and your children's future.

Be aware of which characteristics you share with your parents. These will include positive and negative traits. Look at both the good and the  bad, because you are connected with your parents through both. The wish, "I don't ever want to be like my father!" has little chance of coming true because the genetic link is much too strong. It is an old psychological realization: what we push away sticks with us. The most you can do is to make a more intense effort than your parents to make the best of it. In order to do this, you need to look at the negative sides of the family history and say, "I am part of this."

Learn to deal with the points of conflict in your relationship. If the communication between you and your parents is disturbed or if it has ended completely, there must have been a particular reason or an event that prompted it. Perhaps you were put under pressure and quite rightly did not give into it. Perhaps your mother wanted to go on vacation with you and you did not go—which was your right.

Think about this: you still have a lot in common in many areas, just not in this one. Focus your attention on this subject, which is usually very painful. Don't try to resolve it on the phone; one of the parties can always end the communication by hanging up. Do it with a letter, followed by a visit.

In the worst case, you should agree on a "separation for a period of time." Saying, "I will have no contact with you for a year" opens more possibilities than a quarrel in which you say, "I'm never going to see you again!" People who say that feel guilty forever after and they feel bound by it. Time does not heal all wounds; nevertheless, in conflicts among people there is a sort of "statute of limitations" that you should put to use.

Simplifying Idea 22: Prepare for Your Funeral

This simplifying idea might seem macabre. There is, however, a high probability that you won't be as mentally capable in the final part of your life as you would like to be. That's why it really does make sense to give some thought now to the end of your life.

Work out Your Funeral

When you die, your relatives will have to make a lot of important decisions—and they will have to make them in a state of shock. There is a mammoth difference in price between a simple coffin and an extravagant one; it's the same with the other details of a funeral. You can help your family a great deal by writing down a few statements. For example, you could write, "I wish to be buried in my parents' grave in Mount

Ever-Rest Cemetery in a very simple coffin. It would be nice if you could sing my favorite hymn, 'Abide with Me.' Please invite all my friends, after the funeral, to gather at the New Inn and drink a toast to me. You know that my favorite meal was steak and French fries with a beer. Instead of flowers, I would like my friends to make a donation to XYZ. Mourn for me, but do not despair. I leave this world knowing that I have had a fulfilled and happy life."

Make Sure You Can Die with Dignity

Doctors who attend you in the last phase of your life are in a similar position to your relatives: if you can no longer express your wishes, they will be required to do everything possible to prolong your life—even if the situation becomes practically absurd. This is where you can help by having documents drawn up.

The documents to prepare are called "advance directives." This is a general term for two kinds of legal documents—living wills and medical powers of attorney.

In a living will, you document your wishes about the medical treatment you want to receive if you are near the end of life and unable to communicate. The purpose of a living will—which can also be called a "medical directive," a "directive to physicians," or a "health care declaration"—is to guide members of your family and doctors in deciding which medical treatments, if any, they should use to delay death.

In a medical power of attorney, you appoint someone to make decisions about medical care for you if you are unable to do so. The document may also be called a "health care proxy," a "durable power of attorney for health care," or an "appointment of a health care agent or surrogate."

Each state regulates advance directives differently. Most states combine the living will and medical power of attorney into a single document.

As much as we would like to simplify this matter, we must suggest that you contact an attorney or at least consult the American Bar Association Web site, *www.abanet.org*, which provides some guidance and access to forms. You can also find information and get forms through Partnership for Caring, *www.partnershipforcaring.org*.

Arrange Material Things

"Make a will." We find this advice in books again and again. However, a will serves to simplify only if you've discussed it with everyone concerned. Otherwise, you might cause more dissatisfaction with your will than you realize.

In any case, the simplest solution is to give possessions away now. If you want to pass on certain items of value or keepsakes to friends or relatives, then why do this only after your death? Give things away while you're still alive. That way people can thank you and the recipient receives something much more valuable than the object—the personal memory.

Leave Knowledge About the Family

In the future it will become increasingly important, psychologically, to have information about ancestors. That is the reason for the pressing need to write down what you know about your grandparents and other relatives. Your descendants will be grateful to you at some point, even if they do not yet appreciate the value of what you bequeath them.

Simplifying Idea 23: Weaken Feelings of Envy

It makes life unnecessarily difficult for you and for others if you constantly have to compare yourself with people to work out who's better and who's got more. Comparison is not a bad thing in itself, as long as it doesn't result in a feeling that you come off worse than others when you see that you have less and it seems unjust.

Money or looks, a particular talent or reputation—anything can give rise to envy. Attempts have been made on the political level to remove the basis of envy: a society in which everyone owns an equal amount. But envy has continued even there. It is a hidden but stubborn problem that makes life difficult—both for the people who are envious and for the people they envy.

But you can do something about it. In fact, envy can become a source of motivation in your life. Have a look at the simplification strategies for dealing with envy—both in yourself and in others.

Strategies for Dealing with Your Own Envy

Take a look at the real balance of light and dark. People never envy bad things; they are envious only of good things that other people have. You

need to be aware that no one has it good all the time and that a price has to be paid for the good things in life. An envious person wants to have something without paying the price for it. A violin virtuoso

pays for his talent and his fame with countless hours of hard work, frequently associated with a deprived childhood. Do you envy that as well? A person with power and influence has dangerous enemies; she needs bodyguards and alarm systems. Would you really want that?

Use the Esau–Jacob method. Envy is often resentment, not wanting to grant the other person recognition. If you cultivate an attitude of goodwill toward people as a conscious counterstrategy, you will become actually pleased for them. Apply the anti-envy formula as an immediate measure and say to yourself, "I don't begrudge them what they have!" Repeat this sentence again and again in your mind until you can agree inwardly.

A similarly effective way of counteracting envy can be found in the Old Testament: "I have enough, my brother; keep what you for yourself." (This is what Esau says in Genesis 33:9 to his brother, Jacob, who had once cheated him.) This is a very effective way of reducing envy while simultaneously developing a healthy self-esteem.

Develop Goethe's gift. Johann Wolfgang von Goethe pointed out that love is the only thing that helps when faced with other people who have good qualities. You can use this insight to reduce your envy most impressively. Pay other people genuine compliments: for their appearance, their manner, their culture, their style. Transform your envy into praise and recognition (which is what envy actually is, but in distorted form). Your envy can be turned into a personal quality that values everything that is special, good, and beautiful in other people in a positive and authentic way. Make your own very personal gift in this way. People will appreciate and respect you for this attitude.

Use the principle of co-operation. A nagging feeling of envy usually leads to a breakdown in communication: you develop negative thoughts about the other person and you talk to him or her less. Talk to the person whom you envy and ask him or her quite openly and honestly: "This and that is what I like about you. How can people achieve that? How did you manage it?" Or,  even better: work together with the person whom you envy most. If he or she is really good, you can only benefit from working together. Learn from him or her and use your envy as a motivator for success.

Take the creative way. Envy is frequently a sign that you are not giving expression to your creative potential. Use your imagination and allow the fountain of your creativity to bubble forth. Try to do something creative as often as possible: make music, do handicraft work, paint, dance, write. The more clearly you recognize and develop your own talents, the less reason you will have to feel envy. The satisfaction experienced after time spent creatively quickly erodes the feeling of envy.

Live the satisfaction plan. Envy thrives on unfulfilled needs and causes people to be depressed. Develop a willingness to regard every moment of life as fulfilled: everything you need is there—either visibly or as a dormant possibility. Where there is satisfaction, envy and depression don't have a chance.

Simplify. The greater the importance of simplicity in your life, the less envy you have to feel. If you give up your collection of coffee cups, you will not envy other people on account of their more impressive collection. The plain, the simple, the unspectacular—that is the healthy answer for of envious people in their quest for meaning.

Strategies for Dealing with Envy in Other People

Show a healthy pride. Don't let people take away the pleasure you experience in connection with your good qualities, successes, or other positive experiences. Be proud of yourself and express that pride out loud when you are alone. But don't show off. Don't unnecessarily provoke feelings of envy in others.

Show friendly self-confidence. When you encounter envy disguised in compliments, you should retain your self-confidence. Do not belittle yourself or the other person by saying something like "Oh, anyone can do that." Stand by your good qualities and achievements: "Yes, that was a good piece of work and now I'm enjoying the fruits of it" or "Not everyone is having as much luck as I am at the moment. I sometimes have bad times—and that's why I'm feeling so good now."

Don't let people get you down. If someone is envious and uses the old "Oh, that's nothing" method, you should draw a clear boundary. Here's 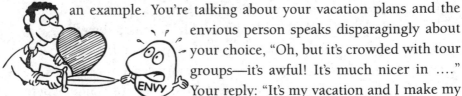 an example. You're talking about your vacation plans and the envious person speaks disparagingly about your choice, "Oh, but it's crowded with tour groups—it's awful! It's much nicer in ...." Your reply: "It's my vacation and I make my decisions according to my own criteria, just like you, right?"

Create clarity with a clear objective. If an envious person has got it in for you to such an extent that he or she really tries to do you damage (harassment, lies about you to the manager, plotting against you, malicious gossip, etc.), you should ask the person to explain, calmly confronting him or her with the facts. Don't make the person's envy the subject of the discussion. (He or she will always deny it.) Look for a simple, pragmatic solution to the problem. Tell the person directly how much this behavior hurts you: "You would find it hurtful, wouldn't you?"

Give honest praise. Help others to get over their feelings of envy by paying them genuine compliments that they really can understand. But don't exaggerate or it will not be credible.

Simplifying Idea 24: Let Go of Anger

One of the biggest factors preventing the construction of a vital social network of friends, acquaintances, colleagues, and relatives is the urge to judge other people (and preferably improve them at the same time). It's not a problem for everyone, but some people are prone to an unhealthy obsession to criticize. In order to live a happier, simpler, and more relaxed life, you should clear out your box of judgments and prejudices, so to speak.

There Is a Difference Between Your Judgment and Reality

American therapists Connie Cox and Cris Evatt have worked out a proven method of dealing with excessive annoyance. It starts with an exercise.

Think of someone whose behavior irritates you again and again. Write a sentence on a piece of paper with the following simple structure:

"_____(name)

should _____."

Don't do this exercise in your head; it's important to actually write something on paper. The more concretely you write the sentence, the better.

Here is the background to this exercise. What causes the mess in our minds is the jumble of *negative* judgments we carry around with us. The sentence you wrote down expresses one of these judgments. It describes how other people should behave: Peter should be more hardworking, John should be more punctual, Susan should stop smoking.

Judgments differ—by their very nature—from reality. Reality describes how people actually behave: Peter is lazy, John is unpunctual, Susan smokes like a chimney.

One judgment gives rise to further judgments. In the example of Peter, who is lazy, it might go like this: Peter is going to fail. He's going to be thrown out of school. He won't get a job. He'll go downhill. He will end up becoming a criminal and a drug addict .... This way of thinking can go on and on in any way. It reinforces the negative orientation of the mind until it dominates and distorts perception.

Free Yourself from the Need to Solve Other People's Problems

Life can be divided into three areas:

1. *Life itself,* in the sense that it is subject to natural laws. The sun rising in the morning, the weather, the fact that you have to die one day: all that clearly lies outside your sphere of influence.

2. *Lives of other people.* This is the area that you addressed in the writing exercise with the "should" sentence.

3. *Your own life.*

The message for simplification is this: concern yourself exclusively with this third area. Constantly looking for solutions to other people's problems can be a dreadful burden. Thinking about possible solutions to their problems weighs upon your mind and soul. Psychologist Jack Dawson points out that there is nothing that simplifies life as much as restricting yourself to matters that you yourself can change.

Judgments About Other People Make You Ill

Read again the sentence you wrote down. (If you have not written anything yet, do it now.) How do you feel when you read it? Does it make you feel happy? Or do you feel anger, sadness, or anxiety when you read it?

As a rule, judgments cause unpleasant feelings, which come under the general heading of stress. And this stress has been brought about by nothing other than your own thoughts! You pay a high price for them, because these critical judgments can isolate you.

While you are thinking critically about someone else, you impair your ability to engage in social contact. Even such a harmless thought like "What an awful pair of pants he's wearing!" brings a flood of further judgments with it. "He doesn't look after himself. He's got such bad taste. He's gradually going downhill. We should keep away from people like that."

Dawson also discovered that people with negative convictions are distinctly worse listeners than people whose views are as objective as possible.

If you talk about the need to deal with the judgmental mind, people often object, saying something like "But people need values and standards." But don't be deterred—people can still behave properly without the jungle of acquired judgments. Rely on nature's power of judgment, on the instinct of life.

Psychologist Jon Kabat-Zinn conducted research and discovered that non-judgmental people make judgments with greater clarity than judgmental people. Non-judgmental people live in accordance with simple ethical principles, they are more effective in their actions, and they are happier.

This Is How You Tidy up Your Mind

Every person has amazing natural abilities that make it possible to live a relaxed and happy life. Those abilities are just buried under a mountain of convictions and dogmas. Here are two simple methods that will allow you to uncover the natural, positive aspects of your personality.

Method 1: Train yourself in healthy questioning. When a chain of judgments arises in your head ("My husband should spend more time at home. He leaves me on my own. He doesn't love me."), just try challenging this sequence of judgments. Is your view really the only possible one? Could it be that someone else would see it differently? Consciously take a completely different viewpoint ("He is wearing himself out working for his family. He wants the best for all of us. He is putting his own needs aside.").

This type of questioning is extremely effective, because it breaks through the endless string of connected judgments. You don't have to cover up the other person's faults; just try to see the facts clearly.

Method 2: Relate the reproach to yourself. Use the word "I" to replace the name of the other person in the sentence you wrote down and especially in your string of judgments. See whether it expresses something on your part: "I leave him on his own. I don't love him. I am just like all the others." Could that be the reason for his absence?

This simple exercise shows you the real purpose of your powers of  judgment: to enable you to assess yourself and grow. Turned against others, judgments become poison. But for you they are medicine. Judgments are supposed to be a remedy, not a weapon. The writer Anaïs Nin put it like this: "We don't see things as they are. We see things as we are."

Accept Reality ...

Let's continue with our example. Your partner is often away. That is the reality. Reformulate the reality—as an experiment again—in the form of a judgment. "It's right for him to be away. It's good for him." Initially, it sounds outrageous. However, in this state of clarity you could ask your partner to spend more time with you—for the first time without pressure, without reproach, and without hidden messages. Now you can leave the decision to him. It's his area of life and you leave it to him. Consequently, order has returned to your thinking—and to your relationships.

... So That It Can Change

Psychologist Byron Katie, who developed these methods, pointed out that when one partner finds a new way of looking at things, the tension in the other partner dissolves. In our example, this would mean that if one partner were to stop criticizing, the other one would give up unconsciously struggling against the reproaches—and would want to come home earlier.

All of this also applies when dealing with children. Parents and teachers usually criticize their own weaknesses in children. Katie's advice is that we should think back to our own childhood and ask ourselves whether anything ever really changed because of other people's judgments ("You should work harder"). Probably not. A young person is not influenced so much by people who judge him as by people who meet him or her without passing judgment, listen to him or her, and believe that he or she is capable of great things. You should become such a person.

This requires patience; there will always be setbacks. But do embark on this part of your way of simplification, even though it may appear impossible at first. The further up your life pyramid you go, the more rewarding the simplification work will be!

The method for letting go of anger applies to all relationships with friends and acquaintances and also for your life partner. We have devoted a whole chapter and a level of the life pyramid to this most important relationship in your life.

Simplifying idea 25: Develop your relationship

Simplifying idea 26: Take the drama out of your discussions

Simplifying idea 27: Balance the relationship between work and private life

Simplifying idea 28: Unlock your sexual energy

Simplifying idea 29: Make joint decisions for your old age now

Step 6 of Your Life Pyramid:
Simplify Your Life Partnership

Your Dream of Simplicity: Seventh Night

There is a further surprise waiting for you on the penultimate level of your life pyramid. The previous and step was loud, lively, and gigantic because you encountered an enormous number of people there. You know that there is only one person waiting for you on the level you are now entering—the person who has a unique place in your heart and you are ready to find that person in a relatively small area.

But as you go up through the levels (or are you carried up?), there opens up before your eyes a lovely landscape that appears endless in the gentle evening sun. The scene is slightly reminiscent of paradise—a huge garden with small hills, winding paths ,and bubbling springs. Creepers hang from mighty trees and the ground is covered with lush green ferns.

As you take your first few steps on the soft grass, you notice that there are faces on either side looking at you. They are not real people, just semi-transparent lights, as though they were projected here from the past. They are all the people whom you have loved and whom you have since forgotten, to whom you said a gentle goodbye or whom you have forcibly deleted from your memory. There is one person who it is very difficult to walk past. You linger for a moment and smile at that person, silently and gratefully.

Then you walk on into the colorful world of your personal paradise—which is not a paradise everywhere, by a long shot. You see thorns and gravel, weeds and garbage. And yet you sense that it belongs to you, just as it is. And you are no longer alone. The person whom you love has been silently walking along next to you for a while now. You reach out a hand and your fingers touch. Then you grasp hands.

At this moment you forget that your life consists of anything more than this moment, for it is the moment that you had long forgotten—when you both stood next to each other for the first time and, without words, in your hearts you both decided to go forward together. You look at each other and open your mouths to say something. But you don't need to say anything. Not now.

Simplifying Objective for Step 6

Learn to look beneath the current surface of your relationship and to continue on your way—together instead of just side by side.

The title of this book, *How to Simplify Your Life*, really means more than simplify your *life*; you could say it means simplify your *lives*. Your life consists of more than just you. Your husband or your wife, your life companion—this is not just another person but a part of your soul. Even if you do not see it on the surface or perhaps don't see it at all— unconsciously you have already grown together. That is why separation or divorce is so painful. Consequently, it is more important to maintain this relationship than it is to look after your objects, finances, time management, body, or social network.

If you have been reading this book on your own so far, you can now give it to your partner. Or you might just happen to leave it open some place which you consider important for your relationship. The time has now come to go the way of simplification together.

Simplifying Idea 25: Develop Your Relationship

Psychoanalyst Michael L. Moeller talks about the current status of marriages and partnerships in terms of the death of the couple. People are unprepared and naïve when they go into a relationship, the biggest risk of their life. They allow too little time for each other and each blames the other. They are absorbed in the outward duties of their life. Sooner or later, they are no longer sexually attracted to each other. One day they find themselves in a state of amazement and despair, in a relationship that seems irreparable.

The reasons are varied, but nowhere near as unique as they seem to the people involved. The social roles of men and women are undergoing a historic change. Women now enjoy an unprecedented degree of freedom in terms of work and on the economic level; they also have to confront an unprecedented dimension of difficulty. The expectations that women have for men have exploded, and yet the other demands from work and other social relationships have not decreased.

Even the expectations that men and women have of themselves have increased dramatically: success in professional life, a lot of free time, independence on the material level, a happy sex life, hopefully staying in love for their whole lives, wonderful children .... There has never been such pressure on couples' relationships as there is today. What the extended family achieved in the past with great effort, the small family is now expected to achieve and more perfectly than ever.

The first step toward solving the dilemma is for people to "essentially" talk to each other. Not about work or the children or food: you need to talk about yourself. Every couple does this at the beginning of their relationship. They are curious about each other; each wants to know everything about the other. Out of the growing intimacy sexual attraction grows. But then each person thinks he or she cannot discover anything more about the other, because they have told each other so much and they know everything about each other. Most relationship problems stem from this error.

The Rules of Dialogue

Moeller developed the practice of dialogue, which has proved successful thousands of times with his clients. It consists of a conversation in which you apply some simple but fixed rules. Both partners commit to follow the rules.

186

Fixed time. Agree on a time each week and an alternate time (in case anything comes up at the regular time) when you can talk to each other undisturbed for 90 minutes—"just the two of you alone."

Fixed procedure. Sit opposite each other, because the important things are conveyed visually rather than by words. Block out any disturbance (telephone, computer, background music, television). Do not shorten or extend the conversation.

Fixed exchange. You need an hour for dialogues. One person speaks for 15 minutes and then the other speaks for the same length of time. The person who listens does not ask any questions, not even to understand.

Fixed subject. Each person talks about the things that are really issues for him or her at the moment. Moeller  talks about it in terms of painting a self-portrait. Each person focuses only on *himself or herself.* If you speak about the other person (which is allowed, of course), it should not be in a judgmental way; instead, you talk about *your own* feelings in relation to your partner. That is the difference between dialogues and quarrels in "relationship boxes," in which each person tries to make the *other one* see what he or she is really like.

Why Dialogues Have Such a Good Effect

Moeller says that every couple lives in a double reality—your reality and your partner's reality. If each person gets to know the other person's reality, the relationship will be enriched. However, if each person wants to convince the other person that his or her own reality is better, the relationship is inwardly doomed. That is why the most important requisite for dialogue is that both realities be equal.

In dialogues, both partners learn the following five great truths.

1. **"I am not you."** You learn that you both know each other much less than you thought. In a long-standing relationship, one partner is always claiming something in relation to the other one. Moeller talks about this in terms of "colonizing the other" or "couple-

racism": each person is secretly convinced that he or she is somehow the better of the two. An honest dialogue puts an end to this.

2. **"We are two faces of one relationship."** At the same time, you learn not to consider yourselves as two independent individuals but as a couple that has been growing together for a long time on the subconscious level. The nature of love is such that it involves the soul. Even your partner's worst qualities belong to both of you. For example, if your partner keeps a secret from you because he or she is ashamed of something, it is not "his or her guilt" alone, since in relation to someone else he or she might not feel ashamed of it.

When you have internalized this basic simplification wisdom relating to a relationship, you will no longer be able to hold your partner exclusively responsible for anything. This insight revolutionizes everyday life in your relationship. There is no longer any basis for blaming your partner or yourself, because you are both involved in anything that either one of you does.

3. **"Talking with each other makes us human."** You learn that you can only change yourself; you cannot change the other person even if you try constantly. You learn that talking with each other brings you into a relationship not only with the other person but also with yourself. The biggest deficiency in most relationships is not "couple poverty" but "me-poverty." One partner expects from the other things that he or she can really only get from himself or herself: self-esteem, satisfaction, confidence about the future, and zest for life.

4. **"We tell ourselves stories in images."** Instead of vague feelings, learn to remember specific scenes. Instead of "I think you're great," you say, "This morning I saw you as you were coming round the corner on your bike with your jacket flapping in the wind and the sun in your hair. I just thought you were wonderful." Even your inner life will

then become richer in images. You will begin to understand your dreams as a joint experience in which each of you gains access to your joint unconscious.

5. **"I am responsible for my own feelings."** You learn to understand your feelings as the *actions* of your unconscious—and not to think that feelings come over you in some fateful way or that they are created from outside you. You learn to express your feelings more clearly and to be more in control in the way you deal with them because you are not governed by every impulse.

When a Dialogue Goes Wrong

Don't give up if your dialogues do not work in the beginning. This is the most common mistake in partnership communication: people give up too quickly. Whatever happens, you should agree to have at least 10 discussions. Just think how tenaciously you have to pursue an objective in your professional life or how often you have to repeat things to your children until they get it. You should also be as patient with the most important person in your life.  Have faith: dialogues optimize themselves. If a dialogue turns out awful, the next one will automatically be better. Dialogues have an effect that goes beyond; as a result, other discussions will also become more substantial and more open.

The Effect of Dialogues

Psychosomatic research has revealed that the human immune system is significantly affected by the quality of couple relationships. Blood counts improve measurably after a dialogue.

A person's subjective feeling of happiness is likewise heavily dependent on the couple relationship.

A good partnership also has a big influence on the couple's children. In later life, each child will unconsciously emulate the qualities shown by his or her parents toward each other.

After a while, the improved communication resulting from the dialogues will also enhance the couple's sex life. It is a mistake to think that good sex is only possible through a feeling of strangeness (a popular argument to justify escapades on the side). Mutual understanding and intimacy are the best ingredients for fulfilled eroticism.

Two Minutes per Day Is Not Enough

A study carried out in 2000 involving 76,000 people revealed that, on average, couples spend two minutes per day talking about themselves. The results of this study were frequently misquoted in the press, as though couples spent only two minutes talking to each other at all. That's not true, of course. What we're talking about here is "substantial" communication, in which the subject is each partner and the relationship. Make sure the figure increases drastically for you!

Simplifying Idea 26:
Take the Drama out of Your Discussions

Why do so many marriages break down? Why are relationships between men and women becoming increasingly difficult? American psychologist John Gray believes that most couples who want to divorce could remain together if they just understood the fundamental differences in the ways men and women communicate. His theory is that men and women are so different that it's like men are from Mars and women are from Venus, which is also the title of his book.

Gray has woven his discoveries into a nice story. Women used to live on Venus and they were always endeavoring to build community and harmony. Relationships were more important to them than work or technology. Venusians were convinced that everything could be improved. They took advice and constructive criticism as proof of love. The Martians, on the other hand, valued creations and achievements. They wanted to achieve goals and they were particularly proud of doing things on their own.

One day the inhabitants of Venus and Mars discovered each other and each group immediately noticed that the other had exactly what they lacked. So the Martians built spaceships, brought the women back from Venus, and populated Earth with them.

Do-It-Youselfer vs. Coffee Talker

Gray's discovery is simple: men and women are fundamentally different in the way they solve problems. For men, problems are there to be solved, alone if possible—like a handyman. However, women see problems as an occasion for communication. Women look for contact with other people to talk to about their problems. But men withdraw.

This difference in the relationship is the basis of countless misunderstandings that can lead to the end of the relationship.

Understanding What the Other Person Means

The situation: One evening a woman talks about her worries, all the work she's got to get through, because tomorrow is the deadline for her article and there are still some important things that need to be done.

Typical (but wrong) reaction: The man talks about the problem and about facts: "Can't you delegate some of it or postpone it till the day after tomorrow?" As "handyman," he doesn't know that his wife's complaint is a request to start a conversation. This is *how the woman takes it*: "You only ever see facts; you never see me."

Here is the right response: He should sit down with her, listen, and agree. This alone would be enough; then she could cope with mountains of work. The woman does not want solutions; she needs understanding.

The situation: The man comes home in the evening and he feels weighed down by the many deadlines and jobs he still has to deal with.

Typical (but wrong) reaction: The woman gives advice and constructive criticism: "You shouldn't take on so much. You've got to take it easier." This is *how the man takes it*: "You don't trust me to do anything."

Here is the right response: She should tell him that he is good and that he will manage it. Then she should leave him to work or relax.

Mars and Venus in the Bible

Gray's basic wisdom is already found in a statement by Paul (Ephesians 5:33): "Each man is to love his own wife as much as he loves himself, and let a married woman see to it that she treats her husband with respect."

In this way he is going against the grain. Men usually have a great respect for what their wives do. There are hardly any men who speak ill of their wives. But men have difficulty with love, feelings, and affection. The contribution that they prefer to make to a relationship is going out, earning money, and doing something that makes an impression.

Women want attention and understanding—especially from their husbands. They interpret too much action as a lack of love. Women feel that their role is to express love and to show feelings. Work and money take second place for them. They find it difficult to regard them as a contribution to a *relationship*.

In contrast, men want recognition—especially from their wives. They love to hear things like "You're great at that." They see well-meant suggestions for improvement as hidden criticism.

The concept of Mars and Venus is also extremely good for reviving relationships that have become stuck. Don't use your knowledge of this as a reproach ("You just reacted in a typical Venusian way again!"). Instead, use it as a tool for self-analysis ("That was Martian language, sorry!"). Include the subject of Venus and Mars in your next dialogue and talk about it with other couples. This is a particularly helpful form of partnership communication.

Learn to Make Requests Properly

A lot of people are frustrated in marriages and partnerships because the other person does not perceive their wants and needs. Sometimes this is simply because they have not asked for what they want. And sometimes the partner appears to ignore the wish quite steadfastly.

This happens in all types of relationships—in marriage, in the family, with friends, at work. Fortunately, there are a few tricks to solve the problem. American therapist Rinatta Paries has compiled them after 20 years of experience in marriage guidance and counseling. This is not manipulation, just simple rules for mutual understanding.

You Are Allowed to Ask

This is the most important tip. Every person has the basic right to say what he or she wants and needs. It doesn't matter whether it's about help in taking care of the children, about food, about money, about advice, or about affection—ask the person from whom you want something for what you want. Always.

Be Prepared for a Yes or a No

Ask in such a way that the other person has a free choice whether or not to fulfill your wish. People love freedom. If you ask an open question without hidden threats ("If you really loved me ...") and without a negative undertone ("I can already sense that you are going to say no"), you will receive a positive reply more frequently than you think.

Accept a "No" Answer

Do not react ungraciously to a negative reply. If you do not remain kind and magnanimous, your request was not really a request: it was a demand. Demands are unpopular and they engender resentment. If you take a "no" answer badly, you will provoke further replies of the same kind. However, if you accept the "no" answer now, you open the way for a "yes" answer in the future.

Stand by Your Wish

If you ask someone for something and the other person does not want to fulfill your wish, don't just let the matter drop. Stay true to the need you have expressed. Don't let the other person talk you out of it.

Have Confidence in the Other Person

Even if you have received a "no" to your request, have faith in the possibility that it might turn into a "yes." You should presume that the other person has no bad motive toward you in declining your request. Perhaps the other person could say yes if he or she were aware of your real reasons and needs. Explain them in a gentle and patient way.

Don't Swallow Your Reaction

Tell the other person what effect his or her "yes" or "no" has had on you. Show your enthusiasm or disappointment, your displeasure or gratitude.

Keep a Balance Between Giving and Taking

A lot of people think that if they guess their partner's every wish, then 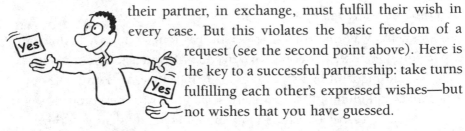 their partner, in exchange, must fulfill their wish in every case. But this violates the basic freedom of a request (see the second point above). Here is the key to a successful partnership: take turns fulfilling each other's expressed wishes—but not wishes that you have guessed.

Don't Nag—Ever

Grumbling or nagging means making the same request over and over again to wear the other person down and make him or her give in. This is often done in a tone of resignation that suggests, "You're pigheaded, you're never going to change." Occasionally, nagging will actually make the other person give in. But it has a high price. The other person does not like fulfilling the wish and he or she does it with a feeling of resentment. If you must repeat a request, don't do it by constantly wearing on his or her nerves; do it according to the rules discussed above.

Appreciate, Appreciate, Appreciate

If you get a "yes" answer, you should really celebrate. Be grateful. Never take the fulfillment of a wish for granted and never regard it as your

earned right. The more clearly you show your enthusiasm and gratitude, the more obliging the other person will be in the future.

Don't Expect Miracles

"Why do I have to ask? Why couldn't you just do it?" Don't be angry if the other person doesn't guess your wishes. He or she is not you. Presume that the other person thinks about you in the same way. You should not imagine that in your partnership or family each person will have a perfect intuition and do what the other person expects. It's better to develop a culture of asking and thanking.

Simplifying Idea 27: Balance the Relationship Between Work and Private Life

We hear people say again and again that work is the enemy of a happy marriage or relationship. The stereotypical complaint from a woman married to a successful businessman is "You don't have any time for me." It is also becoming increasingly common for men to make the same complaint about their working wives. Management and personal coach Günter F. Gross has been interested all his life in the relationship between work life and private life and he has come to a very interesting conclusion: successful people have acquired skills in their work lives that they can also use in their partnership or marriage. Basically, this means that people who are good at their job have a good chance of making their relationship work!

The ingredients for a good performance at work are the basic commodities of time, energy, enthusiasm, and determination—precisely the features of a good life partner. Here are the steps on the way of simplification to make a good relationship with these ingredients.

Revolutionize Your Time Planning

The key element for making work skills usable in your private life is to rethink what you do with your time. It's been proven that 20% of your projects bring 80% of the success. Of course, you  cannot always know in advance which 20% will be the rewarding ones. However, in the case of many projects, you can say with a reasonable degree of certainty that they will be among the unsuccessful ones. There is one advisor who has a better feeling for these matters than you do: your life partner.

That is why the most important rule is that you should allow your partner to help you with time planning more than you have so far. He or she is more rational than all your colleagues. He or she knows the ways in which you tend to waste energy; he or she knows your strengths and your long-term objectives. In your time planning meetings with your partner, ask him or her to refrain from making any emotional comments ("Are you going to that stupid trade fair again?"); instead, your partner should ask you targeted questions like the following:

- Will that be something worthwhile to schedule in terms of future benefit?
- Would you do that even if you were allowed to work only six hours per day?
- Will it benefit both of us?
- Which old projects would you give up for this new project?

Of course, relationship-based time management means spending time for a joint planning meeting. But you can be sure of one thing: those conferences will be the most important of your life! A lot of people go to one meeting after the other—but when it comes to their marriage, they think it will just work by itself without any arrangements.

You need to regard every investment of time in your job as critically as you evaluate financial investments. If your employers could not raise the finances for particular projects, you would never think of paying for them with your own money. Apply the same principle to time issues. Too many people regard their private life as a time resource, which they can plunder without a thought when bottlenecks occur at work.

Your Best Personality Advisor

If you are likely to agree to particular deadlines and projects merely out of consideration for third parties, let your partner give you moral support to say no. Nobody is more able to do that than he or she. Think about this good rule: someone who takes up a project with determination lets go with even more determination.

If, for example, your manager expects you to work evenings or weekends, give a truthful answer: "I'll have to talk to my partner about it first." You may find it embarrassing at first, because it then becomes obvious that you cannot make decisions concerning your time independently. But you are not alone; there are two of you. Now your manager has to find arguments that convince your wife or husband as well.

Instead of Using up Time, Tank up on Energy!

In the joint time planning, don't think just about time that can be measured; it's also worth considering the mental energy that the items on your schedule take—and generate. Making a speech in front of an important audience might cost a lot of mental energy because of stage fright, in addition to the preparation time. But  if it goes well, you will gain self-confidence and energy. Jobs you like to do or that bring you recognition will replenish your reserves. And don't forget: the right type of success also makes you more attractive to your partner!

Don't just take it for granted that you will be dead tired after a 12-hour day and that your private life has to recharge your batteries. Even if it might sound impossible at first, work in such a way that at the end of the working day you come home feeling glad, relaxed, and cheerful.

Arrange your tasks and appointments in such a way that you bring energy into your relationship and your family at the end of the day. An evening with a balanced partner can be nicer than a 14-day vacation with an exhausted partner!

Think of the "Affection Account"

In the long term, a company is concerned with economic survival. That is why it makes profits, invests for the future, and forms reserves. If your company does not survive economically, that also means a disaster for you personally.

It works the same way in a partnership. The important issue there is emotional survival. The factor that determines it is neither money nor profit. The capital of a marriage is affection. Handle this basic ingredient as carefully and intelligently as you handle money in your company. In the same way that you use time and money to generate financial profit at work, in your marriage you should put time into affection.

It is often the simple, silent moments when you refuel togetherness and replenish affection resources—but the moments need to be prepared

in a loving and intelligent way. Surprise your partner: allow yourself the luxury of a bit of love nostalgia. If you have been invited out in the evening, come home a little earlier, make a little detour, go for a little walk where the two of you can look at the moon or an expanse of water glistening in the night. Have the courage to be romantic. Declare your love for your partner. Even if he or she knows it, your partner will like hearing it again.

Simplifying Idea 28: Unlock Your Sexual Energy

The "affection account" consists of romantic moments, loving words, attentive gestures, a bouquet of flowers, and small gifts—but also physical love, of course. This is an item in the "affection account" that suffers especially with people who are successful in business—even if very few admit it. Here are a few simplification remedies you can use if the eroticism has declined and a few arguments to counter outdated preconceptions.

Don't Pay Any Attention to Surveys

Preconception: An international study revealed that American couples had sex most often and for the longest time (20 times a month for 35 minutes).

Wrong! Here's the truth: This result merely reflects the enormous social pressure in the United States. Even when it comes to sexual matters, people need to look really good in comparison with the neighbors and they are quite unrestrained in the way they lie on questionnaires. Californian psychiatrist Linda Perlin Alperstein is sure that there is no area in which people lie as much as they do when they are involved in research about sex. So don't let yourself be stressed by figures about how much desire a man or a woman should have. Go by your inner needs and your partner's needs. Progress in small steps: a kiss at the time of day when you wouldn't usually kiss, a gift without any particular reason, an affectionate handwritten greeting when you are the first one to leave the house in the morning, etc.

Check Your Body

Preconception: The problem with the lack of desire or potency is always in the mind.

Wrong! Here's the truth: You need to talk openly with your doctor about sexual problems. Difficulties in your sex life are often side effects of drugs. A fashionable medicine, St. John's Wort, causes a decrease in sexual desire. Erotic problems may be an indication of organic illnesses, such as a disturbance in the hormone balance (this frequently happens with women after a pregnancy), or it may be a thyroid problem.

One of the main causes of a decrease in sexual passion is lack of exercise. Types of athletic activity in which you really exert yourself and push your performance limit almost automatically bring about an increase in sexual activity—provided you don't take it too far.

Kiss and Cuddle (Again)

Preconception: Sigmund Freud showed us where the erogenous zones of the body are.

Wrong! Here's the truth: The whole body is an erogenous zone that can "turn you on." However, everyone has some "turn-off" places where they don't want to be touched. And the preferences may change over the course of a lifetime. Your partner may have really liked something in your first few years together, but now he or she might just find it a bit silly—yet not really dare to say so. Do a five-minute body discovery journey with your partner. Use your body language or even just a purring noise to show what you like—and don't react too negatively to what you don't like.

Forget about categories like "foreplay" and "the act." Doctors in Asia are convinced that integrated sex (with a fluid transition from kissing and cuddling to sexual intercourse) is not merely enjoyable; they believe that it keeps you healthy and increases your life expectancy.

Get away from the idea that kissing and cuddling has to end with "it"—especially if you have not been having sexual intercourse for some time.

Arrange a Time

Preconception: "Sex has to be spontaneous."

Wrong! Here's the truth: Anticipation is one of the best aphrodisiacs. Remember your first rendezvous: the excitement, the fantasies, even feeling a bit scared—that's all part of it. In the midst of work life and family life, which can really be detrimental to passion, you should plan intimate times just like you do with other appointments, however unerotic this may seem at first.

Be Egoistic

Preconception: Sex needs total mutual understanding.

Wrong! Here's the truth: Couples that live together harmoniously complain about a declining sex life much more than couples that keep quarreling. This is something that sex therapist Bernie Zilbergeld observed. This does not mean that you have to deliberately pick a quarrel. It is enough to just be aware that sex works  best when each person doesn't just think about the needs of his or her partner, but rather thinks just as much about his or her own desire.

Even if you don't think it's necessary after many years together, every man and woman wants to be sexually conquered again and again.

Simplifying Idea 29:
Make Joint Decisions for Your Old Age Now

A lot of people regard life as a continuously rising curve: it's always going upward. People who think like this experience the process of getting older as a disappointment and a crisis, a deviation from the planned route.

In reality, our lifeline is a well-proportioned curve that rises steeply in the beginning: you grow, you learn, your living space increases, you progress in your job, and you might start a family.

In this phase you have big needs: a house or an apartment with enough room for everyone, perhaps a garden or a vacation home, perhaps also some gadgets and other items for your hobby and work. Life is multifaceted and complex. This may also be the case in matters relating to your partnership: separation, new ties.

But one day the children will be standing on their own feet. Your own ability will decrease; you will have a smaller range of activity. Your life will be become simpler and it will occupy less space.

Why You Should Know at 45 How You Are Going to Live at 65

According to a study at the University of Hanover, Germany, more than 50% of all people over age 65 are objectively overextended by their living conditions: an apartment that's too big, a house that's too big, or a garden that's too big. But only about 10% acknowledge the problem. The reason is that learned behavior patterns are very difficult to change when we get older. The decisive changes for a sensible life in old age need to be made earlier. Either things have to get simpler or it simply won't work.

American psychotherapist Myrna Lewis has proven that the critical changes that are significant for your behavior and your mind in old age should be completed before your 49th birthday. After that it will be very difficult to adapt. So, in the fifth decade (40 to 50), you should decide how and when you are going to simplify your life. The most important person for this is your partner. If you omit this important life planning, you are heading for a relationship crisis that is becoming increasingly common: retirement shock.

The Unhealthy Dream About Prosperity in Old Age

In contrast with developing countries, the system of financial security in most Western countries is outstanding (despite the negative press). The result is that people continue with the same standard of living in their old age as they had during their family days: a large house, a big car, great expectations. Doctor and journalist Heidi Schüller says that

we overextend ourselves in old age. The focus of life gets stuck on the material level in an unhealthy way. There is insufficient room for the necessary mental development. Thanks to modern medicine and modern ways of life, people don't have to stop doing things when they get old. People remain mentally and physically fit and they have every opportunity to structure their lives actively, look for new activities, live with awareness, and enjoy.

There is hardly any other area in which the principle of simplification is as important as it is in planning for the third stage of life. Think back to your youth: perhaps you enjoyed it, the simple life when you were studying or learning your trade. You can then use that phase of your life as a model for your old age. Or you can look for examples: old people who are content and whose life experience you can benefit from.

Here is how a plan for the third stage of your life might look:

- When we get older, we will move into a smaller apartment that's suitable for elderly people or we will look for a facility in .... We have a specific age in mind: 70 at the most.
- We don't want to continue to do everything ourselves; we intend to get more and more professional help for the house and garden. The first step will be ....
- We will continue to be active and we are prepared to learn new things, possibly from younger people. The first step will be to start taking a course on the subject of ....
- We would like to have time for essential things and to create opportunities to experience the beauty of life. The first step will be ....
- We want to reconcile with ... now. (We don't want to wait until we're old.)
- To avoid disputes about inheritance, we're making a will now.
- We would like to die in dignity, not as the subjects of long-term geriatric medicine. For this purpose, we have arranged the following with the people listed below, with whom we are on close terms: ...

The way of simplification has become more and more serious. We're not talking about a disorderly desk or worries about money; this is about final matters. This book covers the whole of life—your whole life. We hope that you are now excited about the next chapter. What will be waiting on the highest level, i.e., in the heart of your life pyramid?

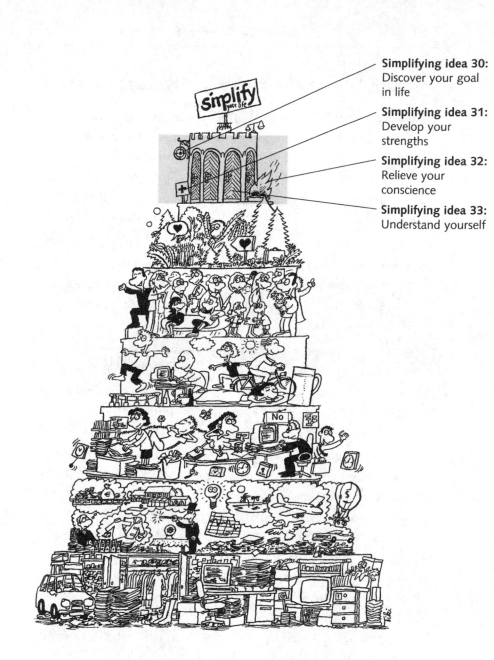

Simplifying idea 30:
Discover your goal in life

Simplifying idea 31:
Develop your strengths

Simplifying idea 32:
Relieve your conscience

Simplifying idea 33:
Understand yourself

Step 7 of Your Life Pyramid:
Simplify Yourself

Your Dream of Simplicity: The Last Night

You were in paradise. You saw that it was like paradise and at the same time rather mundane. You were in a landscape and you sometimes had the feeling that you had reached the peak of your life. But all the time, while you and your partner were wandering around the territory of your relationship, you had a strange urge to take yourself out of the relationship.

At first, you thought it was a crisis. Were you tired of your partner? Did you feel the need for a new erotic adventure? But that wasn't it. It was even stronger than sexual desire, a longing even stronger than the need for another person. It was an indescribable urge to be on your own.

And then you discovered the old tower. It rises out of the mist, rather like the first stage of your life pyramid emerged out of the dawn at the beginning. You quicken your pace. You want to let go of your partner's hand, but then you notice that your partner has not been at your side for a while now. You are alone.

The tower appears like an old temple, like a summer house or a small castle. In places it is overgrown with ivy and climbing roses. It looks very old and yet in many places it has evidently been renovated or completely rebuilt. You walk around the edifice in amazement and you discover that it has nine doors. That makes you curious. The first door you happen to want to open is locked. The next one only opens a crack. You investigate all nine doors, one by one, and you discover that they all look quite different. However, one of them appeals to you more than the others. You carefully place your hand on that door and it opens inwardly, quite easily and without a sound.

It's dark inside the tower. You need some time to adjust to this dark silence. Then you look up and you forget to continue breathing.

The sky arches above you, a starlit night, but it's not like anything you see on earth. This is how it must look in space, you think, and at the same time you sense that you are no longer standing: you are weightless and floating. The inside of the tower is immeasurably large and immeasurably deep. You spread your arms out and it suddenly occurs to you that all the stars in the infinite space of the universe are you.

Then you look down and discover the gigantic crystal directly beneath you. It is a long way down; the distance is indescribable. You are drifting down toward it (or is it coming up toward you?) until you can almost touch it.

Again, the thought occurs to you: it is me. It has my color, my form, my light, my temperature, and my beauty. Even if I am not like it yet, I should become like it. And you know that you are at the destination. No, you have not arrived. But you have seen it, even if you are not allowed to touch it. You know it, but you are not allowed to possess it.

You feel behind you carefully. There is the door. You hold the handle firmly and you are glad that you can feel it. You turn around and step out into the open air. But you don't look at the landscape nor do you look back inside the tower. You just look at the door with a profound sense of gratitude.

Simplifying Objective for Step 7

Learn to understand yourself better and to move toward the purpose of your life.

The tower at the peak of your life pyramid is your "I," your personality, as it was built up and changed, molded, and structured every year and every day of your life. What you have seen inside yourself is something that goes far beyond your individual "I." It is to be found in the deepest core, where you are connected in a unique way and with all other beings and the whole of creation. Psychologists call it the self.

It provides the energy for life. This source of energy (that can be described only through allegories and symbols) nourishes your individual life goal, which we have described here as a crystal.

Simplifying Idea 30:
Discover Your Goal in Life

No one is on this earth "just like that." Each life has a goal; it has its inner purpose. There are 100,000 things that distract you from it day after day. However, when you simplify your life, it means that you at last get a clear view of this goal again. Every person—even someone with the most unspectacular, chaotic, or miserable life—has a goal. It is fed from four sources.

1. Life Itself

You are here to keep life going. This is meant in the biological sense: you have children or you safeguard the lives of other people in some other way. This happens by itself. Nobody is there simply for himself or herself. Even someone who seems to be the greatest egoist has his or her significance in the great structure of life.

This basic reverence for life is something that every person feels. It is just that we often cannot interpret it correctly and so we seek it, as it were, in a roundabout way, in the love of animals, enthusiasm for music, or in a strange certainty that this world will soon come to an end. It is important for such people to discover that they carry life within them in order to pass it on.

2. Your Parents' Wish

When two people want a child, they always connect it with a wish—seldom consciously, but rather usually as directed by their unconscious.

Your parents' wish steers your life in an indirect way, like a message given to you in a sealed envelope that is opened only a few decades later. For example, a child is supposed to:

- continue the family name (frequently the responsibility of the firstborn),
- reconcile the mother's and father's families that have fallen out,
- mend the parents' broken relationship,
- make up for a previous loss (perhaps a child who died),
- complete a parent's unfinished task (perhaps to make a company successful),
- or simply to make the parents happy by his or her presence.

There is sometimes an indication of the (usually unconscious) parental instruction in the first name or pet name given to a child. It is worth discovering the meaning. A woman named Irene (Greek: peace) discovered that she was brought into the world to bring peace to a hopelessly divided family. One man had the name George because he was supposed to conquer the problem of the family's economic failure (which he succeeded in doing), rather like St. George defeated the dragon. Another man had the first name of his father's brother. This man, who was regarded by everyone as an exemplary human being, had been killed in the war. The nephew who now had his name was burdened with an impossible task. It took a long time for him to break out of that situation so that he could live his own life free from the past.

3. Your Talents and Weaknesses

A direction for your life also emerges from the things that you are good at and enjoy doing. Imagine yourself before your birth being prepared by a divine organization team for your special task on earth. Your capabilities are not given to you in ready-made form; you get them as talents that can be developed.

For example, if you are of slight physical build, you must have developed other abilities in your childhood in order to compete with others. You had to become an amusing storyteller, a resourceful person good at solving puzzles, or a musician whom other people admire. And so your strengths and weaknesses give rise to your unmistakable profile with which you try to fulfill your life's task.

4. Your Life's Dream

Every person has a dream, a longing that seems more certain to him or her than reality. It is a vision that is clearer than everything you see before you.

Most people lose sight of their life's dream. They don't trust it. They let people talk them out of it. They let go of it because people have told them they must.

The last stage of the way of simplification is especially about finding this dream again and thus your own life's goal. No one can give you your life's goal from the outside—not your parents, not your company, not your life partner, not your children, not even your religion. You have to discover it within yourself. It might well be in alignment with your parents' wish or your life partner or it may be in line with the principles of your faith. However, you should remain mistrustful with regard to other goals that do not spark any resonance or enthusiasm within you.

Simplifying Idea 31: Develop Your Strengths

One of the key teachings from strategy trainer Wolfgang Mewes, who unfortunately has not received the attention he deserves, is that people who concentrate on their strengths can ignore their weaknesses for the time being. A lot of people believe that they have to work against their weaknesses in order to become successful. That is pointless for two reasons. First, you will merely become *average* if you neglect your strengths. Second, your motivation will inevitably suffer if you focus on your weaknesses.

Just like every company, each person has his or her *special strengths*: this combination of abilities, experience, and know-how can be as unique as a fingerprint. These special strengths also include goals, wishful ideas, examples, models, and visions. They steer your own development (consciously or unconsciously) in a positive or negative direction.

The more pronounced a person's strengths, the greater the weaknesses he or she will have at the same time. Yet we have been too educated that we should deal with what we are *not* good at and do *not* want. It is obvious that a person will never do really well in the area of his or her weaknesses.

My 10 Greatest Strengths

Write down your best abilities here—the best in your opinion and in the opinion of other people, both professional and personal abilities. Do not stop until you have 10 items.

1. _____
2. _____
3. _____
4. _____
5. _____
6. _____
7. _____
8. _____
9. _____
10. _____

Now put an X next to the three strengths you think are most important. These are your key tasks. It is a matter of decisive importance for your strengths that you simplify your overall image of yourself by concentrating on your outstanding points.

If you find it difficult to name your three most outstanding strengths, approach it the other way: put parentheses around the less important ones. Your essential strengths will soon emerge.

My Professional and Private Key Tasks

Ask yourself the following questions:

What do I need to do now in my professional and private life to be *happy* and *successful* (in the best sense of the word) in my opinion? Write down five tasks that you feel have priority.

1. _____
2. _____
3. _____
4. _____
5. _____

Put an X next to whichever one of the five tasks seems to you to be the *most important* at the moment. Ask yourself, "What would help me most quickly to move closer to my ideas of happiness and success?"

Next to each of the five tasks, write the number of months that you will probably need until completion. Ask yourself, "Which tasks do I want to *concentrate* on in the next six months?"

Formulate your core tasks in such a way as to minimize the gap between your work and your private life. Integrate both areas and balance them as well as you can. Be pleased about your strengths and about the fact that in the next six months you are going to use these abilities to fulfill the tasks you have written down, to a greater degree than you ever imagined.

Simplifying Idea 32: Relieve Your Conscience

Guilt and conscience are important products of human development. They are indispensable for a peaceful coexistence. It's horrible when we encounter people who have no conscience, who have no consideration for others. But there is another extreme, which is the point here: people who always feel guilty and whose conscience bothers them about everything, e.g., if they have spent a couple of dollars on something enjoyable, if they have not worked enough, if others around them become ill, or if they decline a request.

If you are one of these people, here are a few simplification tips to deal with exaggerated, unhealthy feelings of guilt.

Identify Your Little Judges

A lot of people who suffer from excessive feelings of guilt have one or more little judges sitting on their shoulder who tell them what's right and what's wrong. It may be the voice of a parent, a relative, a sibling, or someone else who judged them in their childhood or their youth. Take a look at your judges and find out whose voices are speaking to you. Talk to your judges. Tell them that you are now old enough to listen to yourself.

Some people think they are grown up although they allow their inner judges a lot of space. However, the goal of growing up is to become independent of other people's voices. The goal is autonomy, listening to your own inner values and guidelines.

If you later find yourself listening to one of your little judges again, brush him or her off your shoulder with your hand. This ritual helps you to differentiate between your own judgment and an acquired one.

Give Your Judges Some Rest

People who suffer with feelings of guilt frequently work (physically or mentally) to the point of exhaustion and they still feel guilty. Stop before you are exhausted. Tell yourself that you have done your best. Imagine your feelings of guilt as judges again. Put them to bed and say to them, "Even if I were to slave away for another three hours, you still wouldn't be satisfied. That's why

I'm going to stop now so that I will be fresh tomorrow." Then go to bed yourself.

Be Consistent

People with feelings of guilt often live in a disconnected way in several contexts. For example, they are under strain in their marriage but they don't say anything about it at the office—and at the office they are under strain but they don't mention it at home. Then the office judges sit on their shoulder and say, "Don't waste your energy on your private life. Think more about the company!" And in the office the judge is sitting there with their partner's voice and urging them to finish work and go home on time.

Put an end to these unhealthy divisions. Stand by your weaknesses. When you are at home, talk about what you really feel at work. When you are at work, talk about the difficulties in the family. This can be a great relief for all involved—as long as it does not degenerate into gossiping or going overboard in baring your soul.

Accept the Dark Shadow Side of Yourself

People who suffer from guilt feelings sometimes have the feeling that they have to defeat everything bad in their environment. In this way they place themselves under enormous strain. Imagine that all your good deeds inevitably cast a shadow and that you are unable to prevent it.

Find a Trusted Person

Look for someone to whom you can introduce your little judges, so to speak—and who you are sure will simply listen to you without giving advice. It may be a friend, a therapist, or a confessor.

If you don't tell other people what is bothering you and worrying you at the moment, it's a signal that you are ashamed of these things. But you don't need to be, because it's all part of you. Open up to at least one person whom you trust. Tell him or her about your feelings. Don't say, "Oh, I'm not so important." On the contrary! If you reveal more about yourself, you will come across to others as more colorful and interesting.

Think Two Generations Beyond

Imagine your grandchildren (or grandnephews and grandnieces). Imagine that they are going to have the same feelings of guilt and make the same mistakes as you do now. It's not just an idea: it's a proven fact. It is up to you to protect them from those experiences by heeding the rules mentioned above. If you won't do it for yourself, do it for the generations to come.

Simplifying Idea 33: Understand Yourself

The Enneagram—An Answer to the Question, "Who Am I?"

We keep having the same problems, repeating the same mistakes, and failing in the same place. If we could manage to locate the difficulties that typically afflict us, then we would be able to develop very effective counterstrategies that would fit us just right. That is precisely the function of this personality model, the Enneagram (*ennea* is Greek for "nine"), in that it identifies your specific behavior pattern and makes three basic statements.

1. Every Person Has a Life Theme

Every one of us has a particular idea of a fulfilled and successful life. We concentrate our energy on it and we have developed the relevant abilities for it. In principle, there are as many life themes as there are people. However, the many goals can be divided up in an approximate way into nine categories—the nine Enneagram types.

2. No One Is Perfect

As we have already said, the important thing is that you do not blindly succumb to your weaknesses but rather develop your strengths. It will be helpful if you identify your personal Enneagram pattern, for you will

make the amazing discovery that in your greatest weaknesses are hidden your strengths.

Your life theme is like a coin with two sides: positive and negative. Things only come in pairs—you cannot have one without the other. The Enneagram encourages you to develop the positive sides as much as possible and to get the negative ones under control as much as you can. It does not ask anybody to become someone else. It does not demand miracles or that you should become a person without faults and defects. Those are what make people so human and valuable.

3. Each of the Nine Types Has Equal Value

You will lead a happy and fulfilled life by developing the strengths of

your pattern—not by wanting to be a type different from the one you actually are. This is particularly helpful and it reduces tension with regard to your relationship. Consciously or unconsciously, everyone wants his or her loved one to think, feel, and act like him or her—at least a bit. The Enneagram shows with an unsurpassed clarity that two people live in two different realities.

The Small Enneagram Test

How to Take the Test

Fill in the questionnaire in a spontaneous and relaxed way. The main focus should be on the "private you." If you work or have worked, you can fill in the questionnaire a second time from that angle and thus discover something about your professional personality profile.

Give yourself 0, 1, or 2 points:

- If a sentence is *half true* for you, write a 1 next to the corresponding letter in the scoring chart.
- If the sentence is *completely true*, give yourself a 2.
- If the sentence is *not true*, write a 0 next to it.

Test

1. I consider a good appearance, achievement, and efficiency to be important   **f** ☐

2. Other people sometimes think I am unapproachable, temperamental, and not down to earth   **g** ☐

3. Relationships are important to me and I invest a lot of love, time, and money in them   **e** ☐

4. I get angry when other people do not exert themselves and do not take their tasks seriously   **d** ☐

5. I find it difficult to ask for something or to decline a request from other people   **e** ☐

6. Being in competition with others spurs me on   **f** ☐

7. It hurts me to see someone suffering   **e** ☐

8. Disdain from other people is deeply hurtful to me   **g** ☐

9. I constantly work on myself and also like to improve other people   **d** ☐

10. I am careful and precise, even with unimportant details   **d** ☐

11. I am resilient and strong and I can endure a lot   **b** ☐

12. I am prepared to take the lead and exercise power and exert influence   **b** ☐

13. I am direct and open and I speak my mind bluntly, regardless of whether it suits others or not   **b** ☐

14. I am a passionate and sensual, full-blooded person   **b** ☐

15. I like to be with important people   **e**   ☐

16. I like to be alone and I often withdraw from society   **h**   ☐

17. I am good-natured, obliging, and affable   **c**   ☐

18. I prefer to be with other people than to be on my own   **e**   ☐

19. Sometimes I have no impetus and am fatalistic and full of resignation   **c**   ☐

20. I am respectable, reasonable, thrifty, and punctual   **d**   ☐

21. I am quick, flexible, eloquent, and charming   **f**   ☐

22. I am sensitive and I often rely on my feelings   **g**   ☐

23. I am multitalented and I frequently do several things at once   **a**   ☐

24. I am warm-hearted and I have community spirit   **i**   ☐

25. I am reserved and I value my privacy   **h**   ☐

26. I sometimes bluff and bend the truth a bit   **f**   ☐

27. I need a lot of time to rest and relax   **c**   ☐

28. I need time before I begin a task and I occupy myself instead with unimportant things   **c**   ☐

29. I need time to make a decision and stand by it   **i**   ☐

30. I like to unmask people who show off or people who are unjust or dishonest   **b**   ☐

31. I like to express myself in symbols and artistic ways   **g**   ☐

32. I find it interesting to keep developing new ideas   **a**   ☐

33. I empathize with other people's problems   **e**   ☐

34. I often feel at one and very connected with nature and with other people   **c**   ☐

35. I am stingy when it comes to giving other people time or money or keeping people company   **h**   ☐

36. I like to enjoy life, but I often allow myself "too much of a good thing"   **a**   ☐

37. I have the feeling of being constantly monitored by an inner critic   **d**   ☐

38. I have good self-confidence, which rubs off onto others   **f**   ☐

39. I have a finely tuned intuition for contradictions and I look for hidden motives behind things other people say or do   **i**   ☐

40. I do not always have the right instinctive feeling for other people   **b**   ☐

41. I often have the feeling that I need to restrain myself for the sake of others and that I cannot give full expression to my energy because they couldn't take it   **b**   ☐

42. I hold back my feelings and am not good at verbalizing them   **h**   ☐

43. I can make great sacrifices for others   **a**   ☐

44. In a situation of immediate danger, I can see very clearly and act courageously and prudently   **i**   ☐

45. I find it easier to say what I don't want than what I do want   **c**   ☐

46. I can think in a market-oriented way and adapt my image accordingly   **f**   ☐

47. I can put myself in the positions of a lot of people and understand all sides   **c**   ☐

48. I can quickly become enthusiastic about something and find what is good in it   **a**   ☐

49. I have melancholic or depressive phases in life   **g**   ☐

50. I place value on a particular way of arranging my areas, clothing, and work   **g**   ☐

51. I love success and don't like to be reminded of failure   **f**   ☐

52. I solve problems by careful reflection   **h**   ☐

53. I like clear rules and I like to know what I can abide by   **i**   ☐

54. I like spontaneous, quick-witted, and optimistic people   **a**   ☐

55. I would like to be perceived as a unique and quite exceptional person   **g**   ☐

56. I cultivate relationships with people of high social standing   **f**   ☐

57. I prefer to talk about my work rather than about my feelings **f**   ☐

58. I often pull myself together and I am tense inside   **d**   ☐

59. I sabotage my own success by constantly asking myself what could go wrong   **i**   ☐

60. I like to make plans for a nice future, but I feel my limitations when I put them into practice   **a**   ☐

61. In times of stress and crisis, I protect myself by adopting a calm manner   **h**   ☐

62. I long for freedom and independence   **a**   ☐

63. I often long for what others have   **g**   ☐

64. I set high standards and live by values that mean a lot to me   **d**   ☐

65. I get involved for weaker people in a generous and helpful way   **b**   ☐

66. When I encounter problems, I prefer to sit them out than to look for direct confrontation   **c**   ☐

67. I like to stand by people with moral and practical support   **e**   ☐

68. I am true, reliable, and loyal with my family, church, or company   **i**   ☐

69. I rate other people according to how threatening they are or are not to me   **i**   ☐

70. I look for intense, exceptional moments in life   **g**   ☐

71. I like being with people who are knowledgeable in my field   **h**   ☐

72. I let others take the initiative   **h**   ☐

73. I cross boundaries and break rules when I don't understand them **b** ☐

74. I try to understand hidden connections **h** ☐

75. I know instinctively what is right and wrong **d** ☐

76. I know a lot and I am always increasing my knowledge by reading and observing **h** ☐

77. I get angry and irritable if I can't show that I am right **d** ☐

78. I am often plagued by self-doubt and I doubt authorities **i** ☐

79. I want other people to feel at home where I live **e** ☐

80. I sense danger and threats before other people do **i** ☐

81. I don't like conflicts and disputes; I'd rather have peace **c** ☐

82. I sometimes feel like I'm an outsider whom others don't understand **g** ☐

83. I sometimes feel mentally exhausted by other people and I get ill **e** ☐

84. I show my vulnerable, tender side only to people I trust completely **b** ☐

85. I find obligations and routine jobs boring **a** ☐

86. Negative things pull me down; that's why I emphasize the positive sides of things and try to cheer other people up **a** ☐

87. If I don't feel close to other people, I become unhappy and I feel rejected and insignificant **e** ☐

88. I don't get enough pleasure, fun, and recreation because of all the work I have to do **d** ☐

89. I achieve the things I resolve to do **f** ☐

90. When I feel harassed or put under pressure by others, I become stubborn and stop doing anything **c** ☐

Scoring Chart

Your points	Type number
a _____	7
b _____	8
c _____	9
d _____	1
e _____	2
f _____	3
g _____	4
h _____	5
i _____	6

Evaluation

Now you can read your Enneagram profile. The more points you have for a type, the more likely it is to be your type. If, for example, you have more than 20 points for type 9 (letter c) and type 1 (letter d) but less than 10 for the other types, then you should give particular attention to the descriptions for Nine and One.

The pattern for which you can give the largest number of positive answers shows the main elements of your own personality and it *could* be your pattern. You can confirm your initial idea as to which one relates to you if the following apply:

1. You were able to give several positive answers to both adjacent points (on the left and right) *on* the circle (e.g., the most points for Nine and quite a lot for Eight and One).

2. You were likewise able to give several positive answers for both the patterns that are connected to your own pattern by lines *within* the circle (e.g., the most points for Five and also several for Eight and Seven).

3. Ask someone who knows you well to complete the questionnaire. The person should answer the questions from the point of view of "This is what I think your response would be." This third-party assessment provides valuable information for determining your pattern and it can be the basis of an interesting discussion.

Orientation Using the Three Centers

The nine types of the Enneagram are divided into three regions: gut, heart, and head. These three so-called centers correlate quite well with the three areas of the human brain.

Greatly simplified, the human brain consists of three layers. In the sequence of their emergence throughout evolution, you can distinguish between the *core brain* (from the reptilian phase), the *interbrain* (of the early mammals), and the *cerebrum* (of the more recent mammals). The designations for these areas of the brain vary. But the division into three parts has proved to be helpful in explaining the functionality of our personality.

Don't let the descriptions lead you to think, for instance, that the core brain is a primitive organ. The human "reptilian brain" is already far superior to the brain of an actual reptile. All three structures also work together as an indivisible whole. But observations have shown that each person relies more on a certain part of his or her brain than on others. This might be inherited or due to experience. Generally, the personal pattern (and therefore the "number" of the Enneagram) emerges with the onset of adulthood, which is around the age of 20.

Gut Center (Types Eight, Nine, and One)

People belonging to these three types are influenced particularly strongly by the activities in their core brain. This oldest area of the brain ensures our primary needs: self-preservation and preservation of the species; it therefore regulates food, shelter, status within the group, territory, and sexuality. The core brain is the seat of our vitality and of instincts. It makes split-second decisions about life-saving reactions on the basis of sensory perception: fight or flight? It makes these decisions by "gut feeling."

If you mainly feel a dull resentment in situations of conflict and stress and if it seems as if the anger and pain sit deep "in your bones," you are most likely a "gut type."

The three types in the gut center have a strong *primal confidence* in the feelings of their core brain, which dates back to the time of the reptiles. From the primitive force of this source, Eights draw their strength  and directness, Nines their persistence and contentment, and Ones their unconditional attitude and accuracy. The core brain has a very special quality. Compared with the other two brain structures, it needs very little storage capacity. The reactions are mostly "hard-wired," don't need to be learned or questioned, and therefore happen very fast.

Gut types tend to view things as a matter of *life and death*. Their theme is "Am I my own master?" If their autonomy is in danger, they defend their *vitality* by three forms of *anger*. For Eights, it is the easily roused anger, mainly directed outwards and given free rein. For Nines, it is the "slumbering" anger, passive aggression through denial and resistance. For Ones, the anger is mainly directed inwards. In order to legitimize their anger, they look for reasons and for people who are responsible and can be blamed.

All three gut types have a well-developed awareness of unfairness and insincerity. Like no other type in the Enneagram, an Eight can fight for the suppressed and deprived, a Nine will mediate between fighting parties, and a One will accept no compromise in his or her effort to improve conditions.

From the point of view of the core brain, gentle feelings mean a loss of control. In times of crisis, gut types tend to see relationships mainly as a *duel*. An Eight asks, "Do you find me attractive?" A Nine asks, "Am I good enough for you?" And a One is testing all the time: "Do you share my value system?" If there are problems in a relationship, a gut type offers a fair fight: "Come and have it out with me!" The *problem* is that gut types tend to assert themselves by putting other people down.

Heart Center (Types Two, Three, and Four)

The interbrain of the early mammals (limbic system) is folded around the core brain like a covering (Latin, *limbus*) and translates the direct instinctive reactions of that part into more flexible behaviors. Simple black-and-white patterns are replaced by more complex shades of different feelings, a massive potential of interwoven polarities of good and bad, love and hate, joy and sadness, anger and happiness. There is some space here for a changing aesthetic, which must be learned anew by each individual. The limbic system contains enough storage capacity for an extended education. This is where all the *emotional ties* reside between child and mother, family, kinship group, tribe, and society. This is also where the fundamental pair-bond between man and woman is anchored.

Of course, gut and head types can also access the social functions of the limbic system, but with heart types they take top priority. The limbic system is the link between our lower and higher brain functions, which is why members of the heart center often feel particularly "open to the world and receptive to others," compared with the "egocentric" lone fighters of the gut center or the "aloof" singles of the head zone.

In situations of conflict and stress, heart types can snap just as gut types do, but they will often describe it as "being overcome by their emotions." They feel as if they were being pulled in two directions at once. A conflict situation awakens an inner conflict of complex opposing emotions in them, much more contradictory than the clear messages gut types experience.

Heart types tend to view things as a matter of *love and suffering*. The main theme is "How is my relationship with others?" In the case of Twos, this question is posed mainly to the outside world and the moods of others are internalized. In the case of Threes, the personal emotions have "gone to sleep." As a result, they imitate the feelings of others effectively as the situation demands. Fours address the question, "What do I feel?" mainly to themselves and they become easily overwhelmed by their own feelings.

If they have relationship problems, heart types adopt a one-sided view of the partnership as a *duet:* "Don't go! Can you feel my presence? What do you think of me? Do you like me?" Heart types long to be valued and appreciated. Their *problem* is that their own feelings are paramount and they lack objectivity. This can easily lead to illusions and delusions.

Head Center (Types Five, Six, and Seven)

The cerebrum is five times as large as the two underlying areas combined. This is where the capability of reflection resides, the observant  evaluation of the reactions of the early mammal and reptile brains. Language, reading, creative processes, calculating, planning, and thinking about emotional affinities, love, religion, destiny, and philosophy all take place here.

The cerebrum, as we now know, can drastically change the organization of the two subordinate systems. Visualizations in the cerebrum, for instance, can help heal physical illnesses and occasionally modify and rewrite emotional memories. Our new brain is lavishly equipped: it maps the structures of the reptilian brain once more, and this "security copy" only uses a tiny part of its capacity.

To repeat: all three centers benefit from the blessings of the cerebrum. But head types often prefer to explore within their cerebrum rather than experience the real world. They are overwhelmed by their internal microcosm and view life as a puzzle that it's necessary to solve.

The head type is mainly governed by *fear.* For Fives, this is the inward-looking fear of the confusing power of their own feelings, from which they would prefer to be uncoupled. Sixes try to separate themselves from their internal fear and project it onto the external world. Sevens project their fear completely onto the outside world and concentrate on the more pleasant alternatives to the internal possibilities. The main theme for all head types is *distance.* Their principal question is "What do I think about this?" This results in various uncertainties.

"How does it all fit together? Am I safe here? What will give me direction? What's behind it?"

In a crisis situation, head types view a relationship as a *double solo*. Being part of a couple is best, as long as each can be on his or her own. The *problem* of a head person is the retreat into himself or herself, away from the dangerous, disturbing, and painful outside world into the endless microcosm in his or her own head. The fear leads to personal protection behaviors, which by others can experience as unloving or hurtful.

Orientation Using the Nine Patterns

The following text is a short introduction to the nine patterns of the Enneagram. When you first read it, you will no  doubt think of some people who fit one description or another precisely. Don't be disappointed if you don't recognize yourself immediately as one of the types. Take your time to let the whole concept settle in your mind and read the descriptions once more a few days later. For most people, everything already becomes much clearer the second time.

One

Here you have a person who wishes to do everything *right* in his or her life. Ones strive for perfection and completeness, both for themselves and for their environment (the perfect home, the perfect relationship, the perfect job). They live their lives according to a superior value system and try to teach others and improve the world accordingly. Ones are serious people, who live for their work and often deny themselves pleasure. If things are going too smoothly and easily, a One can become suspicious. They are convinced that everything has its price. Mistakes or disorder make them uneasy, to the point where they become annoyed.

Their *tender spot* is *anger*, an inner fury that often comes across to others as stubbornness and determination.

Their *gifts* are *persistence, patience,* and *calmness.*

You can easily talk about goals in life with a One. A One is immediately open to the idea that life serves a higher purpose. Ones are interested in political, social, or religious ideas and reforms. Generally, the *life goal* of a One can be described as follows: "I want to renew something."

Each type of the Enneagram is linked to a *symbolic country.* For the One this is *Switzerland.* This does not mean to say that Switzerland is entirely populated by Ones, but rather that the basic energy of this country's mentality is just this mixture of perfection and simmering anger, combined with a certain lack of humor. The facade must be perfect, while the question of guilt is exported. Should any monies deposited in Switzerland originate from dubious sources—well, those are somewhere far away, outside the country.

A classic *literary* figure of type One is *Mickey Mouse,* always eager to do the right thing. Other Ones are *Asterix* and *Don Camillo,* who both have an Eight as companion (*Obelix* and *Peppone*).

The *caricature* of the One is the carping critic wagging his or her finger, who has no writing talent but corrects others for a living.

Two

Type Two people are *helpfulness* personified. They are relationship-oriented, take action on behalf of others, and want to be needed. They vie for confidence and appreciation through flattery and attention.

Their *tender spot* is *pride.* Behind their aim of "being there for others" lies the overriding desire to receive thanks and be indispensable, a subliminal type of egotism. Twos like to exert influence through money: they give in order to keep the other person dependent.

Their *gifts* are *consideration for others* and *humility.* Charities and church communities would be unimaginable without Twos to manage their activities.

The *life goal* of type Two people is *closeness*: "I want to give and receive love."

The *symbolic country* is *Italy*, renowned for its cuisine and its hospitality. Life in Italy is centered around the family, over which the absolutist Mamma reigns in a seemingly gentle manner.

An impressive example of a Two is the hero of the film *The Godfather*. He embodies the merciless nature of the Two: I do everything for you, but expect total loyalty and thankfulness in return. There used to be the figure of the *Little Bad Wolf* in the comics, who was actually a very good little wolf and battled tirelessly to save the three little pigs from his father, the Big Bad Wolf.

The *caricature* of the Two usually shows a motherly woman (the predominant ideal of the woman used to be that of the selfless Two) with a slightly rounded figure, who bakes and cooks for others, does not forget anybody's birthday, and writes lovely letters and packs little packages until she becomes physically or mentally exhausted.

Three

The main concerns of a Three are *achievement* and *success*. Threes thrive on competition and the prospect of success. The effect is what matters, in other words the image: "How was I?" The example of type Three shows that success does not primarily serve the ego, but has a social function. The Three wants success and possessions in order to gain recognition and have friends.

Their *tender spot* is *lying*—not only to others but mainly to themselves. A Three can tell freely invented or embellished stories about his or her own success until he or she becomes convinced that they're true. The relationship concept of the Three has a tragic component, because nobody gains genuine friends on the basis of possessions.

The *gifts* of the Three are *vigor, optimism, depth of feeling,* and the *ability to translate vision into reality*. As part of a team, a Three will find a solution in the most unpromising situations and manage to enthuse others. For this reason, Threes are often born entrepreneurs.

The *life goal* of a Three is to realize visions externally in real life and also fulfill them internally: "I want to build something."

The *symbolic country* of the Three is the *United States*—success, achievement, optimism, skyscrapers, dollars, Hollywood. Whether genuine or just for show, the main thing is that "it works." The downside of the successful and friendly American optimism is the addiction to being Number One. There is no place for losers.

A positive type Three figure in literature is *Robin Hood,* who steals and cheats with great cunning in order to do good—and who in the end succeeds in winning the woman of his heart (an aristocrat, of course!). *Donald Duck* shows that there are, of course, also Threes who are complete failures, but who still cannot give up their ideals.

The *caricature* of the Three is the poser in the flashy car who tells everybody about his salary, the size of the house he owns, and other status symbols, whether they are interested or not: "My wife, my house, my car, my yacht."

Four

Fours are led by their longing. Their life theme is *individuality*—to be different, something special. They have an unerring sense of all that is beautiful, genuinely natural, and extraordinary, but they also suffer from knowing that there is a great deal they cannot attain. As a result, they tend to be oversensitive and susceptible to melancholy and depression.

Their *tender spot* is *envy*, which cannot allow beauty in others. The downside of being different is the need to compare oneself constantly with others.

 The *gifts* of Fours are their *creativity* and the *art of seeing what is special in others*. Innovations in science and culture are often brought about by Fours, who are not afraid to be different and to "think laterally."

The *life goal* of a Four is to restore originality: "I want to create something genuine."

The *symbolic country* is *France*—vive la différence! Here, there is strong resistance to the loud and optimistic Americanization of culture, and a united Europe can be imagined only in a scenario where everybody else acknowledges the somewhat elitist special quality of *la grande nation* without envy. French cooking is *haute cuisine,* which is "high" and superior to others.

The film *Death in Venice* describes the tragic end of an artist who is in love with the past and who encompasses practically all the typical characteristics of the Four.

The *caricature* of the Four is the francophile artist, who wears only black clothes and a purple silk scarf. His darkened room contains a carefully staged setting with wilted roses, an open poetry book, and his own diary.

Five

Fives cherish their *privacy* and like to shut themselves off from obligations and the demands of the outside world. They collect knowledge, systematize, and analyze, maintaining an emotional distance from situations and other people.

Their *tender spot* is *stinginess.* Not only financial, but also with respect to knowledge and especially themselves. Fives do not like to give themselves, their presence, their time, their emotions, or their treasures.

Gifts of the Five are *wisdom, clarity, objectivity,* and *hospitality.*

The *life goal* of a Five is to fathom previously unexplored areas: "I want to get to the bottom of things."

Their *symbolic country* is the UK: from the splendid isolation of the British Isles, the nation's seafarers and archaeologists collected the treasures of the rest of the world. The crowned heads of England always managed to be immeasurably wealthy and thrifty at the same time. The national avarice is evident in its inability to give back something that it once conquered, Northern Ireland.

The best-known literary Five is also English—the hard-hearted *Ebenezer Scrooge* from Charles Dickens' *A Christmas Carol,* who served as the model for *Scrooge McDuck,* also a Five.

The *caricature* of the Five is the bespectacled (and, if male, bearded) scientist, who hides away in the study with books and a PC. The shy Five maintains contact with the outside world exclusively via the Internet. If a Five ever leaves the ivory tower, then it's preferably to travel and capture the wealth of impressions through a camera.

Six

Sixes are loyal, cooperative, reliable, and warmhearted, but also very cautious. They try to protect themselves against danger by gaining the support of an authority (even though they might criticize it). They have  a very fine sense for hierarchies and always like to know who is above and below them, often showing solidarity with the insecure or the underdog.

Their *tender spot* is *fear*. In discussions they often ask, "But isn't there a danger that ...?" They search for security and try to avoid doing the wrong thing wherever possible. It is one of the surprising revelations of the Enneagram that fear is not primarily a function of the heart but belongs to the head center. Fear results from the anticipation of possible danger, which can, in extreme cases, culminate in an apocalyptical view of a world full of conspiracy theories.

The *gifts* of the Six are *reliability*, *trust*, and above all *courage*. If a Six overcomes his or her fear and caution, he or she becomes the most courageous type of all. The great selfless heroes in wars and emergency situations are usually Sixes.

Their *life goal* is to make available the gift of vigilance and caution to the community: "I want to create certainty."

The *symbolic country* of the Six is *Germany*. Industriousness, bravery, and courage when it matters are virtues of the Six. Germans are at their most likeable when they don't rely on "the state" or other security systems, but open up, in advance, new paths in self-reliance and attentiveness.

One good embodiment of the enormous capabilities of the Six is the *Kevin Costner* character in the film *The Bodyguard*. His credo is "Never feel safe." He has an unfailing sense for danger and is prepared to give his life for his charges. *Woody Allen* practically always plays a Six in his roles, most effectively in *Zelig,* which demonstrates in a mischievous way how a Six can adapt to practically any political system and play a secret role.

The *caricature* of the Six is the apprehensive mousy character, dressed in gray or beige, who does not dare to look anybody in the eyes for long. He has problems bringing conversations to an end. He takes pleasure in leading a double life and being a completely different person from the persona he projects.

Seven

Sevens are optimistic, forward-looking, enthusiastic, and fast. Their life theme is *happiness.* They avoid reality and instead concentrate on all the positive possibilities, to which they are highly receptive. Sevens love the extravagant aspect of creation. They want everybody around them to feel OK; they have a hard time saying no and setting clear boundaries for others.

Their *tender spot* is *extravagance.* "More is always better" is their motto; the affluent and fun-loving society is their favorite environment. They tend to overindulge in everything pleasant: they eat so much, work so hard, and take on so much that it becomes unpleasant.

The *gifts* of the Seven are *cheerfulness* and *a holistic, innovative type of thinking,* paired with a *pragmatic sense of what can actually be realized and financed.*

The *life goal* of a Seven is to enjoy life to the fullest and to help other people to do the same: "I want to increase the good things in life."

One well-known Seven is *Peter Pan,* the boy who does not want to grow up and lives in a dream world called Never Land. He can fly—a primal dream of a Seven looking for easy solutions. The comic character *Gladstone Gander,* with his boundless luck, also personifies one aspect of the Seven.

The *symbolic country* of the Seven is *Ireland*—cheery music, high alcohol consumption, and the habit of saying, "It could be worse!" This idea helped the Irish endure the poverty in their country until their uncomplicated optimism finally paved the way to a European economic miracle in recent times.

The *caricature* of the Seven is a playful, cheery character (often with the curly hair of a child) who does not like to be tied down to any particular role. He views life as an opulent buffet from which he can pick at will without having to limit himself. In his job, too, he constantly needs changes and new stimulation, but he needs little sleep. There is far too much to discover!

Eight

The life theme of Eights is *strength*. They are full of energy, direct, and confrontational. They demand respect by their determined approach, which can be intimidating. But they are not so good when it comes to taking punishment themselves. Their strength hides a certain vulnerability.

This *brazenness* is also their *tender spot*. They have little sense of how they hurt others when they cross the line.

Their *gifts* are *resilience* and the healthy *exercise of power*. Eights go through fire for their charges, resist hostility with amazing strength, and can take up the fight for justice.

Their *life goal* is to end weakness, oppression, and inactivity: "I want to fight for good."

The *symbolic country* is *Spain*. Eights want to see blood, during bullfights as well as in the strikingly bloody representations of the crucifixion in that country. Even though there might be uncertainty behind this machismo, the facade of strength must be preserved.

John Wayne created a monument to the Eight in his films as the abrasive, difficult leader, who usually masters crises and saves his people in an impressively simple, no-nonsense fashion. The Eight is beguilingly single-minded: he fights against evil, disregarding hierarchy, etiquette, and his own health.

The *caricature* of the Eight is the bull-necked, broad-shouldered bruiser. He wears short-sleeved shirts even in winter, defying the weather just as he defies all his other enemies. When he meets someone for the first time, he likes to test him or her with a loud "You don't look too good!" At the next meeting, he greets the person with the pleasant phrase, "Nice of you to put in an appearance!" The fact that this is an invitation to communicate that comes from the heart is probably obvious only to people who are familiar with the Enneagram.

Nine

The main concerns in the life of the Nines are *peace* and *contentment.* They value harmony and comfort. They have set habits and tend toward being absentminded and doing nothing. Nines are peaceable and sympathize with everything. They find it difficult to take a stance or make decisions.

Missed opportunities become sins of omission, which uncover their *tender spot,* which is *laziness.* "But I didn't do anything!" is therefore the favorite excuse of a Nine.

Their *gifts* are *reconciliation, making peace,* and *energy.* Once Nines emerge from their comfort zone, they can develop tremendous energy. Many Nines have numerous hobbies and are always on the lookout for new challenges in order to escape the dreaded boredom.

Their *life goal* is to find an environment in which there is peace and room for all: "I want to reconcile."

Baloo the bear from Disney's *Jungle Book* embodies the philosophy of the Nine: forget about your worries and your strife!

The *symbolic country* that comes closest is *Austria.* Happy Austria did not fight any bloody wars, but expanded its territory through the tame strategy of marriages of convenience. The Vienna coffee house, where you can sit all day in front of a nice cup of frothy coffee, is a Nine's sort of place. Another *symbolic region,* is a little farther away, is *Africa.*

The *caricature* of the Nine is the couch potato who moves between TV and games computer, still in his bathrobe, eating chips. A little overweight, a little slow, and somehow always a little too boring.

Arguments Against Typologies

Typologies are always only an aid and each such personality theory provokes objections, some justified and some unjustified. Here are the most frequent objections voiced against the Enneagram and what we can say in response.

"I Think That I Have a Bit of Everything."

This is what many people say when they first read the type descriptions. But each of the nine descriptions contains characteristic psychological observations. The more you look at yourself critically, the more "a-ha" experiences and moments of self-recognition you will have. But you will be able to fully develop your personality only if you find the main theme of your life among the nine types presented.

"Aren't There Any Hybrid Types?"

Actually, the Enneagram typology acknowledge "wings." This means, for instance, that a Seven is more in tune with the characteristics of the two neighboring types, Six and Eight, than with those of the other types. However, the power of the Enneagram model will begin to develop only once you have made up your mind and start working on your point in the configuration.

"I Could Be Three or Four Types."

But you aren't. It's like in roulette, where the ball will always come to rest in one particular slot. Then your inner restlessness will stop and you will know which life theme you need to concentrate your efforts on. If your test results reflect several patterns equally strongly and you still feel that you are stumbling around in the dark, you should return to the section on the three centers.

"I'm a Ten."

After enough observation, every person shows a clear correspondence with one of the nine patterns. Millions of people have now been given advice with the help of the Enneagram. It has had international scientific input and analysis for more than 20 years. Doctors and psychologists have confirmed the system again and again. You can rely on the Enneagram as a proven method of discovering your life goal. Having experimented with a large number of methods, we believe that the Enneagram is the best tool for self-analysis.

"I Don't Want to Be Put into a Pigeonhole."

Don't think of the individual types of the Enneagram as a restriction, but rather as signposts in a labyrinth. Your personality is so colorful and multifaceted that you cannot discover your real strengths and weaknesses without any orientation. Or, if you wish to stick with the analogy of the pigeonhole, the respective pigeonholes are so immeasurably large that there's more than enough room for your unmistakable individuality.

Our Simplifying To-Do List: Get Out and Go!

All personality and motivation experts agree: we do only the things that we write down. You are now familiar with our 33 ideas for simplification. Start working with them within the next 72 hours. Set your personal focus and write down each day what you have done differently in terms of simplification, what you think and feel, and how you intend to achieve your goals.

Your Simplification Diary

There's hardly a better way to enhance your self-awareness and the way you actively arrange your life than the good old practice of keeping a diary. There have been few celebrities who have got by without a diary. Follow these simple rules:

1. *Appealing.* Get a nice, bound diary (not a collection of loose pages or a ring binder) and a pen or pencil that you like.

2. *Private.* The diary is only for you, not for your descendants or to be published for posterity.

3. *Uncensored.* Just let it flow. Write without qualms. Don't correct spelling errors. A diary is not an essay competition. Nobody else is supposed to read it, just you.

4. *Honest.* Don't censor yourself in terms of content. One exception is if you catch yourself lying when you write. The highest priority is to be truthful.

5. *Patience.* Set yourself a period of time in which you are definitely going to keep a diary. The best inner "a-ha experiences" usually come in the first three months.

6. *Mornings.* Write as early as possible in the day. People have found it helpful to write in their diaries when they are fresh in the morning. Find a quiet place to sit, perhaps with a cup of coffee or tea, and don't regard your writing so much as an exercise in looking back but rather as a jump start.

7. *Free.* The first positive effect of the diary, which you will see already after a few days, is that you will no longer see the day ahead of you as a duty or a labyrinth but as a large blank sheet of paper that you can write on.

8. *Trial.* When you start off, try using a vacation diary. Get a nice book and a good pen: you might have bought some at a vacation resort. Write only on the right-hand pages. Fill the left-hand pages later with photos, postcards, mementos, admission tickets, etc.

Reaching Your Goal

From Dream to Reality

At the end of your way of simplification, you step out through the door of the tower on the seventh level. You look back at your life pyramid and a strange calmness comes over you.

The steps up the individual levels are shaped in such a way that they form an impressive staircase straight from the ground to the peak. The way of simplification has ordered your life into a unique work of art. You realize that the chaos in your life seems to have followed a secret plan right from the beginning: a plan that was already there but that you're just now seeing for the first time. You slowly descend through the levels. It is easier than you expected. You go up a few levels again and laugh. You can glide wherever you want. Your life has become more accessible, the mist has scattered; everywhere there is daylight and fresh air. You start to dance on the large staircase.

At the end of the way of simplification, your life will not be perfectly organized right down to the last detail. You will still have money problems and stress from time to time. You will still get ill sometimes. Things won't always go smoothly with colleagues, relatives, or your partner. But your life is no longer a chaotic entity governed by pure chance; it is a transparent construction in which you will no longer go astray. Individual chaotic events will no longer throw you off the track or cause you to start doubting everything.

You now have enough methods and tools on hand to deal with mishaps, uncover buried doorways, and find inner peace in times of stress, for you have discovered that your life is not a heap of stones but a stable pyramid—your own distinctive pyramid.

Get Out of Your Cocoon

The Butterfly Phases of Your Life

It is useful to imagine the stages of the way of simplification as the phases in the life of a butterfly. After the arduous existence of a caterpillar in which you spend most of your time taking things in (e.g., education and training), you first experience a painful intermediate stage of pupation (e.g., a crisis), and then a relaxed new life with new butterfly wings (e.g., a higher position at work). You will go through such butterfly phases several times—not on every step of your life pyramid, but on those that are the most complicated for you.

Some people think that the life of a butterfly is only very short compared with life as a voracious caterpillar. However, for a lot of types of butterflies, it's the other way around: after a short but intensive caterpillar phase and after pupation, they live a long life as butterflies. Some types of butterflies cross whole continents like migratory birds, covering thousands of miles.

A lot of caterpillars do not make it to the stage of pupation and the development of colored wings. The life of a caterpillar is extremely pleasant and satisfying in its own way. It has its own dynamic. You will certainly know people who warn you against dreaming big. They want to make you see that the different, freer life of butterflies is meant only for a few chosen caterpillars.

The way of simplification ensures that you do not die as a caterpillar. That's why it is important that you discover your potential for getting butterfly wings. We will now go through the phases in sequence.

1. From a Small Caterpillar to a Big One

The motto for the first phase of the way of simplification could be "More is always better": the caterpillar's life in which we learn, take things in, and grow. "Complify" could also be a suitable term, because the way of simplification is never simple in the beginning.

2. The Big Caterpillar

The second station on the way of simplification is an experience on the threshold. We trip over our own ideas. What will become of my life if it keeps going on like this? Is this really all there is?

People who die as caterpillars have not reached the goal of their lives. In this phase the hunger for simplification grows: a bit less would be very good. So where are you to begin?

3. The Pupation

The third phase is about your decision. A lot of people remain caterpillars because they are afraid of change. They do not want to leave the comfort zone. A caterpillar has only one chance of becoming a butterfly: the great crisis, the small death. Only those who dare venture into the darkness achieve the goal of their life, those who let go and enter the pupation phase.

4. The Emerging Butterfly

"Simplify" is the caption for the easy life of a butterfly. Less is more. It flies with light baggage, takes only liquid nourishment, and enjoys freedom. This fundamental attitude could be described as healthy egoism. A film would end here: the butterfly flies into the setting sun and the scene fades. But the way of simplification is not at an end. Simplifying means more.

5. The Butterfly and Its Eggs

Butterflies come into the world to lay eggs. It is not the caterpillars that lay eggs; it is the grown, developed insects that have gone through the big crisis that master the art of flying. That is the great secret of our life, which makes it so exciting and unpredictable.

Use the Butterfly Principles

When you begin a new project, when you want to make a dream come true, when you begin a new phase in your life in any way, prepare yourself mentally, applying the following rules.

Active Instead of Passive

Act, don't react. Formulate your goals in an active form. *Not* "I would like to be promoted to department manager" *but* "I would like to manage the department and transform it using my own ideas."

Be the Director

Become the scriptwriter and producer of your life, not just an actor or a bit player. Express your goals in a descriptive way. *Not* "I want to take a trip down the Nile" *but* "I'm gong by boat to discover Egypt and the Nile."

Feel Your Wings

Have faith that there are undiscovered capabilities lying dormant within you, your butterfly wings, which you can develop and use. The essentials do not come to you from outside; they reside within you and they just need to be awakened. Express your goals as the development of existing talents. *Not* "I would like someone to teach me Spanish" *but* "I am going to develop my knowledge of the language to the point where I can speak Spanish fluently."

Include Your Partner

One of the biggest problems in making changes in life is that a partner may not go along with it. A woman who wants to return to work after bringing up children finds her husband unsym-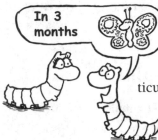pathetic. An employee who wants to work for himself does not get any support from his wife. This is where the butterfly technique can be particularly helpful. Explain to your partner that the butterfly phase follows the arduous caterpillar period: greater satisfaction, more sense of meaning in life, probably also a better income. Set a point in time by which the caterpillar phase will have ended and your partner can breathe a sigh of relief. If the lean period lasts longer than agreed, your partner might ask you to change your plan.

Pay the Price

There are a lot of unproductive dreams of fortune: winning the lottery, getting an inheritance, "being discovered"—inner or outer wealth without effort. The butterfly technique teaches you that there is no reward except through effort. However, it also teaches that effort always brings reward. If you experience the arduous existence of the caterpillar all your life, you are doing something wrong. After a period of exertion, there must always be a positive compensation.

The Five Ways to Develop

As the designer of your life you have five basic options. Put an X next to the ones that seem most suitable for you.

Evolution

There are activities, habits, and areas of work that you can change fairly easily. Complaining, moaning, or getting angry are patterns of behavior whose energy you can use in developing a new, positive habit. For example, you might endeavor to move into a new area of work within your company or you might make a move in your house, making your workroom into your bedroom and vice versa.

Revolution

Ask yourself, "What helps me to find myself? Which conditions prevent me from living in my own identity?" Discover which strengths for a new beginning are lying dormant within you! *Here are some examples:* you give up the job that weighs you down and get a new one that helps you develop your abilities and gives you some vitality, you move into a new house or apartment that's better suited to you, you swap a member of staff who is continually getting you down.

Reduction

A lot of people who actually have a positive, happy nature overfill their life with activities and obligations. In this case, the caterpillar phase may consist of getting rid of superfluous things so that you can take off more simply and easily as a butterfly later. *Here are some examples:* you resign from committees and advisory bodies, you give up a hobby, you give away all the objects you have not used in the last two years.

Addition

In contrast, people who carry out their daily routines in a very controlled way and are afraid of change can best enrich their lives by beginning something new without giving something up. *Here are a few examples:* you learn to play a musical instrument, you learn a foreign language before going to another country, you accept an honorary position.

Metamorphosis

Rather like a caterpillar changes into a butterfly, you can (with a little imagination) transform things in your life. *Here are some examples:* you redefine your type of work or the department in your company and make an extensive change in the work environment with colors, plants, and a rest area;

you dress as you like without worrying what others think; you continue your current occupation but under quite different, pleasant conditions; or you just silently appreciate the new view of your life as an distinctive, unique, beautiful pyramid.

Recommended Reading

Step 1: Simplify Your Things

The American classic for order in the workplace is by Stephanie Winston, *Getting out from Under* (New York: Perseus Publishing, 1999).

For clearing space in your home, we've found the most suggestions in Karen Kingston, *Clear Your Clutter with Feng Shui* (New York: Broadway, 1999).

Step 2: Simplify Your Finances

The most intelligent books on dealing with money properly and attitudes toward the subject of money are those by Suze Orman. Begin with *The Courage to Be Rich: Creating a Life of Material and Spiritual Abundance* (New York: Riverhead Books, 1999).

A good motivational book with many suggestions for seeing everything differently is Richard Carlson, *Don't Worry, Make Money: Spiritual and Practical Ways to Create Abundance and More Fun in Your Life* (New York: Hyperion, 1998).

Step 3: Simplify Your Time

Here we must admit to a bias. But it is a simple fact that Lothar J. Seiwert's books are the best-selling in Germany on the subject of time management. The classic, which has been translated into 20 languages and sold over a million copies, is a must: Lothar J. Seiwert, *Managing Your Time* (London: Kogan Page, 1989).

On the way to becoming a classic is Lothar J. Seiwert, *Wenn Du es eilig hast, gehe langsam*. This book has not been translated into English, but you might try Lothar J. Seiwert, *Time Is Money: Save It* (London: Kogan Page, 1991) and Stephen R. Covey, A. Roger Merrill, and Rebecca R. Merrill, *First Things First* (New York: Simon & Schuster, 1994).

Anybody does not even have the time to read a book on time management should manage at least Lothar J. Seiwert, Horst Müller, Anette Labaek-Noeller, *30 Minuten—Zeitmanagement für Chaoten*. Since this book has not been translated into English, you may want to read Ann McGee-Cooper and Duane Trammell, *Time Management for Unmanageable People* (New York: Bantam, 1994) and/or Jeff Davidson, *10-Minute Guide to Managing Your Time* (Indianapolis, IN: Alpha Books, 2000).

Finally, for those who have lots of projects on their hands and need a way to complete them effectively, we recommend *Managing Multiple Projects* by Michael Tobis and Irene Tobis (New York: McGraw-Hill, 2002), which shows how to keep several balls in the air at once.

Step 4: Simplify Your Health

The easiest way to remain healthy, in our experience, is developed in Gert von Kunhardt, *Keine Zeit und trotzdem fit: Neuer Schwung für Ihr Leben*. This book has not been translated into English. Instead, you may want to read Matt Roberts, *Fitness for Life* (London: DK Publishing, 2002). If you have no time to fit fitness into your schedule, you might try Linda J. Buch and Seth Anne Snider-Copley, *The Commercial Break Workout: Trim and Tone Two Minutes at a Time* (New York: Prima Lifestyles, 2002) or Bonnie Nygard and Bonnie Hopper, *Gotta Minute?: The Ultimate Guide of One-Minute Workouts for Anyone, Anywhere, Anytime!* (Bandon, OR: Robert D. Reed Publishers, 2000).

The undisputed specialist on happiness is the articulator of the concept of "flow": Mihaly Csikszentmihalyi, *Finding Flow: The Psychology of Engagement with Everyday Life* (New York: Basic Books, 1997).

If the issue of water made sense to you, you can find it all in Fereydoon Batmanghelidj, *Your Body's Many Cries for Water*, 2nd edition (Falls Church, VA: Global Health Solutions, 1995).

Step 5: Simplify Your Relationships

Life management is the art of bringing together in harmony work life and private life, including health and all social relationships. The new standard work on this subject is Lothar J. Seiwert, *Life-Leadership*. Unfortunately, there is no English version. An alternative recommendation might be Hyrum W. Smith, *The 10 Natural Laws of Time and Life Management* (New York: Warner Books, 1994).

A good tip for getting along better with others is the DiSC personality model. The nicest presentation, completely illustrated in color, is Lothar J. Seiwert and Friedbert Gay, *Das 1 x 1 der Persönlichkeit*. However, since there is no English translation of that book, you might try Tom Ritchey and Alan Axelrod, *I'm Stuck, You're Stuck* (San Francisco: Berrett-Koehler, 2002) and Julie Straw, *The 4-Dimensional Manager* (San Francisco: Berrett-Koehler, 2002).

The thoughts about clearing out judgmental thoughts come from Connie Cox and Cris Evatt, *30 Days to a Simpler Life* (New York: Plume Books, 1998).

Step 6: Simplify Your Marriage or Romantic Partnership

If you read German, you can find everything about the wonderful technique of dialogue in Michael Lukas Moeller, *Die Wahrheit Beginnt zu Zweit*. Unfortunately, this book has not been translated into English.

The brilliant metaphor of Mars and Venus for communications between men and women comes from John Gray, *Men Are from Mars, Women Are from Venus* (New York: HarperCollins, 1992).

Unsurpassed for the relationship between occupation and personal partnership is the bestseller by Günter F. Gross, *Win at Work and at Home!* (Cambridge, England: Director Books/Woodhead-Faulkner; Englewood Cliffs, NJ: Prentice-Hall, 1991).

Step 7: Simplify Yourself

The background for many of our thoughts about the subject of "inner judges" and life's work is the systematic psychotherapy of Bert Hellinger. The most readable collection of his thoughts is Bert Hellinger and Gabriele ten Hövel, *Acknowledging What Is: Conversations with Bert Hellinger* (Phoenix, AZ: Zeig, Tucker & Theisen, 1999).

If you would like to get into the Enneagram in greater detail, we recommend the marvelously loosely written standard work, Richard Rohr and Andreas Ebert, *Discovering the Enneagram* (New York: Crossroad, 1990). There is also Andreas Ebert and Marion Küstenmacher, *Experiencing the Enneagram* (New York: Crossroad, 1992).

If you would like to use the Enneagram in business, you may want to read Helen Palmer and Paul B. Brown, *The Enneagram Advantage: Putting the 9 Personality Types to Work in the Office* (New York: Harmony Books, 1998).

Index

Index

Index

About the Authors

Tiki Kustenmacher was born in 1953. He is a Protestant minister who also trained as a journalist. Since 1990 he has been working as a freelance cartoonist, author, and columnist and he has published over 50 books. Together with his wife Marion Kustenmacher, he is the chief editor of the newsletter simplify your life®. They live with their three children near Munich, Germany. E-Mail: tiki@tiki.de. Internet: www.simplify.de.

Professor Lothar J. Seiwert was born in 1952. He is a bestselling author who is also regarded as the leading expert in time and life management as well as being the most sought-after coach in Germany. His books have been translated into 20 languages and his work as a trainer and speaker have won him many prizes. His coaching and consulting company Seiwert-Institut GmbH in Heidelberg, Germany. He specializes in the subjects of time management and life leadership®. E-Mail: info@seiwert.de. Internet: www.seiwert.de.